W9-BVE-850

IMPROVING YOUR MULTIPLE STAFF MINISTRY

Anne Marie Nuechterlein

IMPROVING YOUR MULTIPLE STAFF MINISTRY

How to Work Together More Effectively

AUGSBURG/MINNEAPOLIS

IMPROVING YOUR MULTIPLE STAFF MINISTRY
How to Work Together More Effectively

Scripture quotations, unless otherwise noted, are from the Revised Standard Version of the Bible, copyright © 1946, 1952, and 1971 by the Division of Christian Education of the National Council of Churches.

Library of Congress Cataloging-in-Publication Data

Nuechterlein, Anne Marie, 1954–
   Improving your multiple staff ministry : how to work more together
more effectively / Anne Marie Nuechterlein.
     p. cm.
   ISBN 0-8066-2422-1
   1. Group ministry. I. Title.
   BV675.N84   1989   89-30879
   253—dc19   CIP

The paper used in this publication meets the minimum requirements of American National Standard for Information Sciences—Permanence of Paper for Printed Library Materials, ANSI Z39.48-1984. ∞™

Manufactured in the U.S.A.   AF 9-2422

00   99   98   97   96   4   5   6   7   8   9   10   11   12   13

Dedicated to my family:
my husband, Dana
my parents, Nick and Audrey
my siblings John, David, Bruce, and Carole
my sisters-in-law, Kimberly, Paula, and Tammy
my grandparents, Edwin and Marie
and in memory of my grandparents, Walter and Leila

CONTENTS

PREFACE

Have you ever wondered about the dynamics that contribute to satisfactory and enjoyable parish staff relationships? Why is it that members of one church staff have excellent relationships with each other while similar members on another staff have terribly painful and destructive relationships? Based on a qualitative research study involving in-depth interviews with 40 members of multiple staffs, which is explained in greater detail in the appendix, this book addresses these questions by examining staff relationships theologically and systemically. The staff relationships examined in this book accurately reflect the feelings and experiences expressed by the staff members during my interviews, but the names and identifying details have been changed.

A theological reflection on staff relationships is just that. How does faith in Christ make a difference in the quality of your relationships with each other? How does recognizing your hope and holiness in Christ impact your staff relationships? How does covenant-making with God and your staff enhance your staff relationships? Practically speaking, can God really impact your self-esteem, your use of power, and your communication style? If so, how?

A systemic look at a staff relationship entails looking at your staff as a system. A system is a collective whole that is much more than just a group of individuals. What are the dynamics of your staff system? What are your staff system's roles, rules, communication and conflict styles, and uses of power? In what ways can an examination of staff systems enable staffs to function more satisfactorily?

By reflecting on staff relationships from a theological as well as a systemic perspective, various pieces of the puzzle—"how to cultivate good staff relationships"—will be examined. Achieving good staff working relationships involves many components, and it is only when all these components are combined that successful and satisfactory staff relationships are possible. Through reading and reflecting on these vital components of staff relationships, you will discover new understandings about yourself and your staff relationships. As you read, you are invited to reflect on how you can enhance your self-confidence, skills, and leadership ability in your own ministry and in your staff relationships.

Appreciations

For contributing to my theological and psychological understanding of multiple staff ministries, I am grateful to the large multiple staff with whom I work at Wartburg Theological Seminary—President Roger Fjeld, Dean Duane Priebe, the faculty, staff, internship supervisors, and students. I am particularly appreciative of my colleagues with whom I teach in the ministry division—Durwood "Bud" Buchheim, Norma Cook Everist, Daniel Olson, and Ralph Smith, as well as my colleagues in contextual education—Rebecca Bauman, Daniel Olson, and Winston Persaud.

I am thankful for the rich, stimulating, and growth-producing experiences that I have had with the people with whom I have worked in multiple staff ministries: Ken Rogahn; Alton Donsbach and Carol Fight; Keith Palmquist; Robert Breen, Jean and Bob Goodson, Ted Karpf, Jarratt Major, and Charles Walling; and F. Leslie Conrad, Ying Chii Kuo, Pablo Nesler, and Linda Young.

I am indebted to the numerous members of multiple staff parishes throughout the country who participated in my research. Their openness about the issues in their staff relationships helped shape my understanding of staff ministries. While certain details have been changed to protect their identities and in some instances similar situations have been combined, their stories are represented in the characters in this book.

My editor, Irene Getz, offered helpful assistance throughout the process. I am grateful to Patricia Holman, Rollie Martinson, Judith McCall, and Pamela Read, who provided critical evaluations, helpful suggestions, and wise insights. I am appreciative of Gary Harbaugh's useful feedback on chapter 6, as well as Patricia Holman's excellent contributions to chapter 12.

Most of all, I am thankful to my husband, Dana Thalheimer, for his support and presence in my life and ministry.

In our journey of faithfulness with God and with others, we find not one partner but many partners. None of us is single. We are partners with a host of family, friends, and acquaintances at work, down the street, and around the globe. It is only with these co-travelers on the road to tomorrow, and not alone, that we will be able to join God in creating life in the midst of a despairing world.

Letty Russell, *The Future of Partnership*

1

CULTIVATING GOOD STAFF RELATIONSHIPS

t was another one of those days at First Lutheran Church. Loud voices came from the senior pastor's office during his meeting with the associate pastor. Todd Swanson, age 64, a deeply caring and committed pastor with strong opinions, a gruff exterior, and a "soft," gentle inside, was screaming, "You cannot change our worship! I don't care what you learned at seminary. I'm the senior pastor, I've been here 22 years, and I know better than you do as to what's best for this congregation." Karee Lange, age 30, also was a kind and caring person, who usually did not disagree with Todd. Yet her voice was thunderous, "I've had enough. I'm an adult, and a pastor with good ideas. You're treating me like an 11-year-old child. I'm just not going to work at a place where I can't do anything on my own." Pastor Swanson yelled back, "As long as you're here at my church as my associate, you will do exactly what I tell you to do."

Laura Gentry, age 42, the church secretary, overheard the ruckus. Laura was a direct, assertive, friendly, and thoughtful woman who saw herself as "Pastor Todd's secretary." As the confrontation grew louder, Laura thought to herself, "Here we go again. Soon another associate will be leaving."

At this point, the senior pastor's office door flew open. Karee stomped out, looked at Laura, and rolled her eyes. Laura smiled sympathetically at her as Karee stalked out into the hall that led to her office.

Walt Jacobs, age 27, the lay professional in charge of youth and education, was flexible, easygoing, not easily ruffled; a humorous and playful man. When Karee slammed the main office door, he grimaced, knowing that Karee and Todd must have had another fight. He waited a few minutes and then gave Karee a call to see if she was okay. Karee began talking rapidly with Walt. "He wants to tell me exactly what and how I'm to do everything. He acts like this is *his* church and the only person that he'll trust to do anything is himself. He won't talk *with* me—just *at* me."

Walt was silent and Karee's voice was quieter, "Generally I like working here and I enjoy what I do. We work okay together, but I have a hard time respecting him as a colleague." Walt said he understood, and then Karee said, "Anytime I try to talk with him about problems or questions I have, he just doesn't listen. He lectures me for an hour about something that would take five minutes to discuss." Karee thanked Walt for listening and hung up. In a short time, Karee came out of her office, told Laura that she was going to the pastors' text study early, and left the church building.

Before Laura had a chance to begin another project, Pastor Swanson came out to the secretary's office and sat down. Todd sighed, shook his head, and said to Laura, "She acts like she knows everything, and she doesn't want to listen to what I've learned here in these past 22 years. She has excellent skills and we could really work well together, but she wants to do things her way and doesn't care about what I can teach her."

Laura had worked with Pastor Todd for 12 years and with Pastor Karee for 2 years. Todd, as senior pastor, was clearly in charge of the staff. Reflecting on how many associates had left First Lutheran after only a few years, she boldly asked,

"Pastor, what do you think is going to happen?" Pastor Swanson responded, "She has good skills and does good ministry in many areas of the church. And she's especially good with some of the things that I'm not so good with or interested in; women and social concerns, for example. We could work well together if she would listen to me and if I could trust her to do what I say." He then told Laura he needed to get some more work done prior to leaving for the weekly text study.

Across town at First United Methodist, Associate Pastor Marie Reilly, Senior Pastor Ed Mantig, Youth and Education Director Sheila Simons, and Secretary Jean Townsend were having their weekly staff meeting. Marie, age 29, had been at First United Methodist just one year and it was her first call to a parish. Marie was prim and proper, reflective, seemingly aloof, assertive, quite bright, and willing to face conflict head-on.

Ed, age 63, had served in many local, state, and national church positions, and had been at First United Methodist nine years. He was quite warm and personable, open and flexible concerning the needs of others, agreeable, strong in his personality, and a conflict avoider.

Sheila, 37, had been at First United Methodist for four years. She had a tumultuous childhood and had spent her 20s working through the pain and difficulty of growing up in a dysfunctional family. She did not enter the ministry until she was in her 30s. She was honest, passionate, artistic, sensual, personal, and thoughtful.

Jean, 43, had worked at the parish for 14 years. She coordinated the majority of the administrative tasks of the parish. Jean was gregarious, nurturing, efficient, highly responsible, trustworthy, honest, and quite capable.

The staff had just about finished their two-hour meeting when Marie asked them, "What shall we do for the Lenten worship series next spring?" Ed turned to her and said, "Why don't you plan next year. It's your turn to decide." Marie looked at Ed a bit surprised, hesitated, and then said, "Well, okay."

The meeting continued but Marie kept thinking about Ed giving her full responsibility for planning Lent. She observed that as his trust in her had developed, he was beginning to let her make decisions and be in charge of areas that were previously in his realm. While she had only preached once a month in her first six months at the parish, Marie was now preaching every other Sunday. She also observed that she was routinely making decisions in her areas of responsibility without first consulting Ed. Marie thought to herself, "I couldn't have found a man who would be easier and better to work with. He's the perfect age, solid and secure enough in himself not to be threatened by me, and full of integrity. I have high regard for him and appreciate the working relationship we have. We may not be good friends socially, but we work very well together."

Ed also found his attention wandering as Sheila, Marie, and Jean talked about the upcoming youth retreat. He had surprised himself by asking Marie to plan next year's Lenten services, but then he realized that he viewed her as a colleague in the fullest sense of the word. Allowing her to coordinate the next year's Lenten worship series truly symbolized Ed's trust and respect for Marie's abilities. He thought to himself, "She's very capable, we work well together as a team, we complement each other. I'm very pleased with the work she's done and I couldn't ask for a better associate."

Ed's attention was drawn back to the meeting when Sheila started distributing the program materials and schedule for the youth retreat. After the four staff discussed some of the specifics concerning the program, Sheila asked if anyone had any suggestions concerning the upcoming retreat. Ed said, "No, I'm pleased with how you've handled the past retreats and it seems like this one is quite well planned." Jean said, "The parents have been very positive about these retreats." Sheila thanked both of them and then looked at Marie, who remarked, "The list of counselors looks good, but you might need an additional counselor if more youth register." Sheila welcomed their support as well as their recognition of her as a full colleague. She appreciated not having to get permission from them concerning the specific details of the retreat, and she thought about how much she had grown during her years with the staff.

Jean left the staff meeting with a good feeling. She thought of how well Ed and Marie worked together. Marie was turning out to be quite responsible, competent, and dependable. She thought, too, of how Sheila had blossomed into an adult who was enjoyable and capable in her own right. She liked working at First United Methodist Church and liked feeling an essential part of the staff.

As you know from your own experience and from the illustrations of the staffs at First Lutheran Church and First United Methodist Church, good staff relationships are developed through a combination of many factors. Each of the issues examined in the following chapters can be compared to a spoke in a wheel. Just as a wheel needs all the spokes in order to be whole and well functioning, so a staff system needs all the skill and relationship pieces to fit together in order to be a complete, functional system (see figure 1). Relationship "spokes" such as faithfulness, forgiveness, clear expectations, communication skills, high self-esteem, shared power, gender, and system dynamics must be understood and developed so the staff "wheel" will function as optimally as possible. All of these components are intricately connected and necessary for good quality staff relationships to be nourished and sustained.

Good Quality Staff Relationships
Many Spokes Working Together

- Female/Male Dynamics
- Becoming Aware of
- Developing Positive Self-Esteem
- Establishing Covenants
- Discussing Expectations
- Using Power Effectively
- **Good Quality Staff Relationships**
- Understanding Staff as a System
- Acquiring Honest and Open Communication Skills
- Understanding Own Family System
- Assessing Own Negative Communication Problems
- Seeing How Family Systems Are Re-created in Work System

Figure 1

2
RELATING AS A
FAITHFUL AND
FORGIVEN STAFF

A s people of God, it is only fitting that God is the center of our staff relationships. No one would disagree with this, yet few of us know how to make this a reality in our church staffs.

Trusting in the power of the Holy Spirit and making a covenant with God and with each other are good places to start. Staff relationships are more likely to be satisfactory if the staff members base their relationship on a commitment to God and to each other. If we commit ourselves in specific ways to God and to each other, expectations and goals can be more clearly articulated and understood. Also, when a staff negotiates the details of their working relationship in the form of a covenant, then loyalty, trust, and open communication can be more easily established and staff members can experience what it means to relate with each other as a faithful, forgiven, Christ-centered staff.

Senior Pastor Ed Mantig, Youth and Education Director Sheila Simons, and Secretary Jean Townsend had terrible relationships with each other for the first six months they worked together. When Sheila joined the staff, Ed and Jean had been working together for five years and had a comfortable working relationship. Associate Pastor Marie Reilly was not yet on the staff.

When Sheila joined the staff, she was unsure of herself. She was put off by what seemed to be Ed's uncaring way of relating to her. She also felt Jean resented her and saw her disrupting what had been a comfortable staff relationship. Ed was disappointed that Sheila had such a strong need for affirmation and support, and he felt burdened by her insecurities. Jean was angry that Sheila required so much of her time, and resented the way Sheila's coming had significantly changed the nature of the staff.

After a particularly serious argument during one staff meeting, they realized that they needed to resolve their dissatisfactions and frustrations if they were to continue working together. Ed knew about a staff which made a covenant with each other on a yearly basis. He described their covenant-making process, and asked Sheila and Jean if they would be interested. They agreed to explore the idea to find out what was involved in covenant making, and to consider making a covenant with each other.

What Is a Covenant?

A covenant is a pledge of our commitment in a binding agreement, made in trust and faithfulness, to God and to our staff members. The prophet Jeremiah speaks of God making a new covenant with us where God will be our God and we will be God's people. This new covenant will be written on our hearts. We will know God as Lord of our lives and God will be the center of all we experience. Jeremiah sees this covenant as a symbol and a hope of God's forgiveness.[1]

To make a covenant as a parish staff involves: (1) responding to God's promises of hope and forgiveness; and (2) making a commitment to the people of God with whom we've been called to work.

First, a covenant is a holy and sacred commitment that God initiates with us that offers hope and forgiveness. Before we can make a covenant with other staff members, we need to identify and commit ourselves to God in Christ Jesus, the initiator and upholder of all covenants. We need to respond to God's covenant by believing that God has called us in holiness to work in this particular setting and with these particular people.

Second, our staff relationships with one another are enriched when we trust that God has called us to work together and to make commitments to one another in Christ Jesus. When we commit ourselves to one another and to God in faith and trust, we view our staff relationships in a more sacred way. We each take more seriously the nature of our commitments to one another and to God, and, in an intentional manner, live out what it means to be a staff working together as the faithful, forgiven people of God.

In order for a covenant among staff members to be as helpful as possible, we must first believe that Jesus Christ, who is the core of any covenant relationship, died and rose for us for the forgiveness of our sins. We are truly forgiven people called to relate to each other as faithful, forgiven people. In a covenant made in the presence of God, integrity and faithfulness to God and each other as forgiven people are essential. As honesty, trust, and loyalty are experienced, faithfulness can be developed toward each other and toward tasks and responsibilities which are mutually agreed upon. Responding faithfully to God's covenant significantly influences how a staff works together. A covenant reminds us of what we are called to be about as we serve together as staff members, and as people of God.

Covenants are dynamic. They change with the ever-changing people who enter into them. A covenant needs to be renewed periodically (the early Christian Essene community renewed their covenant every Pentecost) and reestablished every time there is an addition or subtraction of a staff member. As Ed, Sheila, and Jean discovered, the staff system changes dramatically each time there is a change in the staff membership. Ed,

Sheila, and Jean established a covenant with each other and renewed it on a yearly basis (each wrote one part). When Marie joined their staff one year ago, each staff member took the opportunity to think through in a disciplined manner what this addition meant for each of them, their commitment to each other, their common goals and understanding, and their expectations for their life together as faithful, forgiven staff members and colleagues in Jesus Christ.

The beauty of a covenant is that it enables us to (1) remember Christ's forgiveness for us, (2) focus on God's power to bring faithfulness to our staff relationships, (3) make clear our mutual expectations so that we can have common goals, and (4) hold each other accountable in an honest yet loving way for that which we have agreed to do.

How Do We Make a Covenant?

Covenant making is part of a process that involves both clarification of needs and expectations as well as agreement on common objectives. As people of God and as a staff, we covenant to

1. believe in the hope and forgiveness of Christ;
2. remember we are holy;
3. listen to each other;
4. discuss individual and group expectations;
5. discuss and set common goals;
6. interact intentionally with each other; and
7. promote honest and open communication.

Covenanting together can help build credibility among staff members by establishing lives of commitment and accountability with regard to common tasks, goals, and standards. Such credibility can lead to trust and hope.

Believing in the Hope and Forgiveness of Christ

As clergy and associates in ministry, we are broken people who suffer from feelings of insecurity and inadequacy. Like Ed,

Jean, and Sheila, we tend to think of our own needs before we think of the needs of others. We get carried away with our own agendas. We like being looked up to or being in charge; we experience hurt and anger when we do not feel that we are respected and cared for by our fellow staff members. There is hope for our staff relationships because we have hope in Christ Jesus, who initiates and sustains a covenantal relationship with us and offers us complete forgiveness for our brokenness and failings. When Ed, Jean, and Sheila took the time to discuss their personal faith in Christ and their beliefs in the freedom, hope, and forgiveness that Christ offers, they began experiencing God's forgiveness, faithfulness and hope in relationship with one another.

Letty Russell, a contemporary theologian, discusses how hope in God and in others is central to how we work as partners with each other. Ed, Sheila, and Jean found hope in God's gift of faithfulness even though they did not have any guarantees. They also discovered hope for their staff relationships by looking at how God joined them together in a common hope in Jesus, even though they were unique individuals.[2]

Remember We Are Holy

Each of us has been sanctified and made holy in Christ Jesus. To be holy is not something that we can strive for or attain on our own, but rather something which is a gift from God. God in Christ makes us holy—today, tomorrow, and in all our future days. But we need to remind ourselves and each other of God's gift of holiness. And we must let God continue to renew us in holiness—through prayer, the sacraments, relationships, and times of quietness and celebration. Staff relationships work best if we remember that God calls us to be holy and is constantly working in us to make us holy. We may not always feel that we, or our colleagues, are indeed holy, and we may not always act holy; however, God says that even as we are, we are holy!

Paul Bauermeister, a pastor, a former seminary professor, and currently a psychologist in private practice, speaks of "Habits Toward Holiness."[3] He states that while our holiness is a gift from God, there are habits to be cultivated that help us experience our holiness. Bauermeister suggests that we develop particular habits to help us live as holy people of God:

- contrition (recognizing remorse and regret)
- repentance (asking for forgiveness)
- receiving forgiveness (knowing grace and freedom)
- compassion (caring for others)
- witness (reminding ourselves and others of God's grace)
- prayer (asking God to assist us in our holiness)
- conversation of the faithful (practicing holiness)

When we covenant to develop habits of holiness toward God and one another, our relationships with God and our staff are enhanced. As Ed, Jean, and Sheila vowed to cultivate habits toward holiness, the focal point of their staff relationship was on being holy people of God in Christ Jesus. This was accomplished through weekly devotions and prayer with and for each other. With holiness in Christ central to their staff relationships, they were able to rise above their insecurities and frustrations and to strive to see each other as forgiven, holy people of God. A key to good staff relationships is just that: interaction with each other as faithful, forgiven, holy, Christ-centered people. Thus, a commitment to be holy and seek habits of holiness with one another is vital to God's covenant with us and our covenant with our staff members.

Listening to Each Other

When staff members really listen to each other, each one feels heard and taken seriously. While it may seem unnecessary to talk about a staff making the commitment to listen to one another, my research indicates that staff members generally feel that not listening to each other is one of their biggest problems (see the appendix for more information about the research study). When we do not listen to our fellow staff members, we are not being faithful to God or each other. One dimension of a truly faithful, forgiven, Christ-centered staff is genuine, attentive listening.

Listening involves giving another person careful, patient attention. Listening involves being quiet and taking time out from all of your own thoughts to be fully present with another person. Listening involves your heart, mind, body, and soul—and eyes as well as ears. Listening involves being sensitive to another person's feelings, thoughts, and perspectives.

Such attentive listening is modeled for us in the story of Mary, Martha, and Jesus in Luke 10:38-42. Martha received Jesus into her home and bustled around serving him, while Mary sat at his feet and listened to his teachings. Martha resented the fact that she was busy doing all the work while Mary was just sitting around, and she complained to Jesus. Jesus told Martha that she was anxious and troubled about many things, but only one thing was needful and that was what Mary had chosen to do—to listen.

To listen is to give another person our full, undivided attention. Mary sat at Jesus' feet. She did not try to carry on a conversation with him while she was doing five other things, but rather she gave Jesus her complete attention. It is hard for us to listen to Jesus or to other people if we are not quietly sitting or standing in one place. To listen is to focus all of our attention on being with another person, rather than trying to listen while thinking about or doing other things at the same time.

God empowers you to covenant with each other on your staff and to commit yourselves to listen to one another as Mary modeled for us. Listen to Jesus and to each other with your whole being. In your staff relationships, dare to be a listener. Dare to take time to be quiet and attentive to your fellow staff members. Dare to wait, to be still, to be receptive, to focus on another person's thoughts and feelings while temporarily laying your own personal agenda aside.

Discussing Expectations

In order to best experience staff relationships in a faithful, forgiven, Christ-centered community, staff members need to discuss their expectations concerning their staff relationship with each other. Otherwise, dangerous and painful misunderstandings can develop.

A useful tool for discussing expectations is found in research by Dennis Kinlaw, adapted by Norman Wegmeyer.[4] They suggest that most staff relationships fit into one of four structures: dependent, independent, interdependent, or collaborative. My research has found that most staffs fit into one of the first three structures.

The *dependent* style is hierarchically oriented and one in which the senior pastor determines the objectives, goals, and decisions of the staff and the congregation. The staff members are viewed as assistants to the senior pastor and the senior pastor is clearly the one with authority, in charge of everything. The members of an *independent* staff go their own ways and have their own separate, clearly defined areas of responsibility. They do not meet or talk on a regular basis and function independently of each other. The *interdependent* staff meets regularly for conversation, support, and discussion of their ministry together. Goal setting, decision making, leadership, and ministry tasks are shared by all the staff. They talk openly with each other about their struggles, conflicts, hopes, and experiences in their ministry together.

While it may seem that the interdependent staff structure is ideal, that is not necessarily true. The ideal staff structure is that one which the staff members expect and prefer. For example, Todd, Walt, and Laura all preferred the dependent staff model and worked well together prior to Karee's arrival on the staff. With Todd in charge of goal setting and decision making, they were efficient, effective, well-organized, and felt good about all that they were able to accomplish. When Karee joined the staff, she had a clear desire to work either interdependently or independently and not have her goals and decisions determined by the senior pastor. Todd strongly preferred the dependent staff model and knew it worked well for him. Their staff relationship became difficult because of the different desires and expectations they had for the structure of the staff.

Discussing and Setting Goals

All staff members have goals for themselves and for their ministry, although very often those goals have not been specifically identified. Taking the time to reflect and discuss personal and professional goals that relate to your staff position can enhance your working relationship as a staff centered in forgiveness and faith in Christ. In particular, goals related to theology and ministry need to be discussed.

First, staff need to talk about their theological visions and goals. While it is not imperative that staff members hold similar theological beliefs, it is helpful to have some common theological understandings.

For example, Todd, Walt, and Laura all had similar theological understandings of how they needed to obey and try to measure up to God's laws and commandments in order to be good and faithful Christians, while Karee believed that God loved her just as she was and she could do practically anything and still be a good, faithful Christian. In Todd's mind, Karee's preaching and teaching reflected this more "liberal" understanding of God and her theology made him a bit nervous and uncomfortable. While Karee and Todd had a difficult relationship for many reasons, their theological differences contributed to the uneasiness and the discomfort they felt with each other.

Significant differences in theological understandings can get in the way of effective staff relationships. It is important to talk about beliefs and faith in the early stages of staff relationships. Staffs with a similar understanding of basic theological beliefs are better able to set common goals and establish a shared vision for their ministry together.

Second, a staff needs to discuss goals for their ministry together. A staff with common goals and expectations for ministry is better able to work together because they share a common purpose. With common goals, the energy and effort of the staff members are focused in the same general direction.

For example, Ed, Marie, Sheila, and Jean had common goals for their ministry and worked well together. They had similar expectations and preferences for their staff structure. They wanted to interact with each other in a personal and regular way, and share in the leadership, decision making, and plans for the ministry. When asked to discuss their ministry goals, they all spoke of the importance of worship, pastoral calling, youth, and education.

Staffs with different goals can work well together, but more energy and concerted effort are required. If one of the staff members strongly prefers a different model of interaction or has ministry goals quite different from the rest of the staff, the staff will not function as smoothly.

Intentional Interaction

Staffs can relate as a faithful, forgiven, Christ-centered community more easily when they have intentional interaction. Staff members need to covenant with each other concerning two types of interaction: business and social. Business interaction involves regularly scheduled planning meetings where all the staff discusses various tasks, programs, and schedules. Social interaction involves time to listen and share with each other, and time to talk with each other personally. Social interaction does not need to be a family or evening activity, but rather can be over coffee Monday morning, lunch on Wednesdays, or a breakfast meeting.

Weekly business meetings are nonnegotiable for good staff relationships, while weekly social meetings are recommended but not imperative. My research shows that staffs which meet on a weekly basis to plan, and on at least a biweekly basis to socialize with and support each other, report a better level of functioning than those who don't meet regularly.

Karee, Todd, Walt, and Laura talk about how their relationships as a staff suffered tremendously when they stopped meeting together. They believed that their staff relationships would have been better if they had covenanted with each other to meet weekly for planning, and periodically for socializing. As it was, without a specific covenant with each other to that end, no staff member could hold another accountable to meet and some found excuses not to attend the meetings that were held.

Communicating Honestly and Openly

It is necessary to covenant to communicate honestly. When staff members are feeling angry, hurt, or vulnerable, it is easier to disregard or repress those feelings than to discuss feelings honestly. Ignoring negative feelings is easier in the short run because you do not create any obvious tension or problems among the other staff members. In the long run, however, the lack of honest expression of thoughts and feelings will damage the staff relationship. Negative feelings that are not discussed do not disappear, but are stored up and expressed in subtle or not-so-subtle ways later on.

While we know intellectually that it is far better to communicate openly with each other, a covenant pledged in faithfulness through the power of the Holy Spirit reminds us of the utter necessity of honest communication. Pledging to each other in the presence of God, we are empowered by God to strive toward better communication. A mutual pledge enables us to hold each other accountable and thereby facilitate the process of open and honest communication.

Putting the Covenant in Writing

Empowered by God, your staff covenant has the potential to bring your staff members together in an exciting commitment of mutual trust, genuine caring, and faithfulness. In order for this to happen, the covenant must be put in writing. A written covenant facilitates greater understanding of the expectations and goals of the staff members, as well as enables the staff to better relate as forgiven, holy people in Christ. Covenant writing involves:
1. making a rough draft;
2. discussing each staff member's rough draft covenant ideas;
3. describing each person's areas of responsibility; and
4. making staff goals specific, achievable, and measurable.

Making a Rough Draft

It is helpful to write out a rough draft of your own needs and expectations prior to the formal covenant-making discussion with the other staff. In taking the time to write out your ideas for covenanting with your staff, you would have an opportunity to give serious thought to your specific goals and thereby be better equipped to have a lucid, focused discussion with other staff members concerning your mutual expectations.

The pastoral and program staff members at First Lutheran made a covenant with God and each other. They began the process by first reflecting on their own needs, goals, and expectations, and then making initial rough drafts that they shared with each other. Karee's rough draft was:

My highest priorities for my areas of responsibility are in the following five areas. My specific needs and expectations are:

1. *Leading liturgy*—ideally every week.
2. *Preaching*—ideally twice a month, but once a month would be acceptable.
3. *Youth ministry*—I don't want to be actively involved and would prefer that Walt be completely responsible for it.
4. *Hospital calling*—I would like to share on an equal basis.
5. *Committee responsibilities*—I would like to be fully in charge of half or a third of the committees, and not to have to attend the committees that Todd or Walt coordinate.

I have a lower priority and interest in the following five areas. I am somewhat flexible and open concerning my involvement in these areas, and would be willing to negotiate with the staff concerning their needs and priorities in these items:

1. *Educational ministry*—I would enjoy involvement with adult educational programming, confirmation, and training of teachers; I have less of an interest in Sunday School, Vacation Bible School, and the Christmas program.
2. *Social concerns*—I would prefer not being involved in the community outreach programs, world and local hunger

programs, etc. I would be more willing to participate than to coordinate programs.

3. *Administration*—I am not wild about administrative responsibilities and would be happy not having any administrative tasks. I am willing, however, to share in these areas (the newsletter, general parish correspondence, etc.).

4. *Pastoral calling*—I am open to sharing new member calling, shut-in calling, and general parish calling. I don't have a strong preference in how we divide up these areas of calling.

5. *Evangelism*—I have fears about evangelism, but know it's important and am open to being involved in it.

Discussing Each Other's Covenant Ideas

A staff needs to set aside a fair amount of time to talk with each other about the specific elements of each staff person's goals and expectations. An effective covenant cannot be made unless all staff members are clear about each other's goals for their ministry together. Good understandings of each other's needs may require conversations over the course of several weeks. Effective listening is an important element of this phase of the covenanting process.

Describing Areas of Responsibility

Write out how you perceive the various dimensions of ministry to be shared and divided. Be specific about your goals and expectations. What are your priorities in your staff position? Write out how you perceive your job description.

Is your goal to coordinate and train lay leaders to work with the youth and not attend youth events yourself? Are you expected to be at youth meetings? Do you expect particular staff to attend certain functions? Who do you expect to coordinate the newsletter? How are preaching and leading worship shared? Who preaches on holidays? Who is in charge of stewardship? Who is expected to go to which meetings? Which staff

33

make pastoral calls? How many pastoral calls are expected to be made each week? How are administrative tasks handled during vacations and illnesses?

Making Your Goals Specific, Achievable, and Measurable

As you write down your goals and expectations, be as clear and focused as possible. The more specific you are concerning your goals, the easier it will be for you to articulate your goals to your co-workers and work toward having common goals as a staff.

Goals must also be achievable. If your co-workers cannot envision how your goals can be achieved, they will have a difficult time working toward those goals with you. If your goals are not realistic, it will be difficult to attain them.

As you and your staff set goals, make sure that you can measure them. As you write down your goals, think about how you will be able to ascertain whether you have reached your goals.

After the staff at First Lutheran discussed their initial rough drafts and ideas concerning their expectations of their areas of responsibility, they each made their goals as specific and concrete as possible. Karee's goals and expectations were:

1. *Preaching*—to preach twice a month, and every other Christmas, Easter, Confirmation Sunday, Pentecost, and Thanksgiving.
2. *Youth ministry*—to supervise Walt's work in youth ministry, and attend a youth event/meeting every two months.
3. *Hospital calling*—to share with Todd and Walt on an equal basis.
4. *Liturgy*—to share with Todd and Walt the leadership of liturgy every Sunday.
5. *Committees*—to be in charge of three committees, to have Todd be in charge of three committees, and to have Walt be in charge of three committees wherein we each have full responsibility for the committees we chair.

6. *Committee attendance*—not to attend committee meetings that Todd or Walt chair.

7. *Weddings and funerals*—to take turns doing weddings and funerals with Todd, so that we share equally in these important events and are both seen as fully functioning pastors.

After all of the pastoral and program staff (Todd, Karee, Walt, and Laura) discussed their own specific goals and expectations that they had written, they started talking and negotiating with each other. They talked about each of their goals, and made decisions concerning how various areas of the parish ministry would be shared. They put these decisions in writing, and prayed that God would empower them to be faithful to God and to each other as they sought to live according to their covenant of mutual trust, respect, and holiness.

Summary

A covenant made with God and your staff members is a solid component of a good quality staff relationship. By reminding yourself of how Christ empowers you for a hope-filled, forgiven, and holy life, you are better equipped to listen, discuss expectations, set common goals, interact intentionally as a staff, and communicate honestly and openly with each other.

By intentionally putting your covenant in writing, you are able to be particularly clear about your mutual commitment and accountability to each other as a faithful staff in Christ Jesus. Through the power of God, a written covenant facilitates staff members to more consciously relate with each other as forgiven, Christ-centered people. Remember, though, that covenants are not etched in stone. Every time there is an entry or exit of a staff member, a new covenant is necessary. For large staffs, this might necessitate recovenanting two or three times a year. Plan a periodic review of your written document, and plan to revise it as your staff membership changes.

Good quality staff relationships begin with commitments to God and to each other. Staff relationships are further enriched by being clear about your role expectations and the qualities that you prefer in your co-workers. Chapter 3 will examine the importance of knowing your role expectations and the characteristics that you value in your staff members, as well as the different co-worker qualities valued by senior pastors and associates.

3
IDENTIFYING ROLE AND STAFF EXPECTATIONS

A s part of the covenant process, you and your co-workers clarify expectations of one another. It is quite likely that you as a staff member have clear expectations and preferences concerning the characteristics that a senior pastor, assistant minister, youth director, music director, secretary, or other staff member should possess. Your staff relationships are enhanced by your awareness of the expectations and qualities that you and your colleagues desire in each other, as well as by your ability to discuss your preferences with your co-workers.

Expectations

Staff relationships are influenced by the role expectations that staff members have of each other, and of their staff relationships as a whole. The quality of staff relationships is often determined more by each member's role expectations than by the actual qualities that any given staff member brings to the ministry.

For example, Senior Pastor Todd Swanson's whole life revolved around his parish. His entire ministry had been at the same parish, and he usually worked 60–80 hours each week. Todd expected Associate Pastor Karee Lange and Lay Professional Walt Jacobs to have the same commitment. Karee put in the required amount of time, while Walt worked many 12-hour days.

Karee expected to have full responsibility for certain areas of ministry, but she found that Todd had to approve everything. She felt that Todd revised many of her ideas and programs because he thought he understood the parish and its needs better than she did.

Conversely, Walt and Laura expected to work as assistants to Todd. They expected Todd to formulate the goals and the vision for ministry, while they assisted in carrying out those ideas and plans.

Todd, Walt, and Laura had fair staff relationships. While none of them would have described their situation as ideal, their roles and responsibilities were in line with their expectations. Todd and Karee had a poor staff relationship because they had different expectations of what their roles would be in their work together.

The expectations we bring to a staff are conditioned by many factors. We may have prior staff relationships that "worked great," which we expect to reproduce in our current staff. Like Karee, we may have specific needs which we hope will be met by our relationships at work.

How we view relationships in general has a bearing on our expectations. If we have a hierarchical picture of working relationships, like that of Todd Swanson at First Lutheran, how we envision things working out differs dramatically from the expectations generated by a peer relationship vision. It is essential to effective staff relationships to share our visions and expectations with one another.[1]

Assessing Characteristics Desired in Co-Workers

In addition to discussing role expectations, a staff needs to consider the characteristics they value in their co-workers. If a staff can recognize the qualities which they appreciate in each other, they can arrange roles and responsibilities to utilize the strengths of each staff member. There are common characteristics that senior pastors and associates prefer their co-workers to possess. The next sections will further examine those qualities that senior pastors and associates prefer in their co-workers.

What Do Senior Pastors Value in Their Staff Members?

While senior pastors could list many qualities that they would like their staff members to possess, my research has found there are three qualities which they particularly value. These are competence, complementary skills, and trust.

Competence

In response to the probe, "Tell me about your relationship with your staff," most senior pastors began by discussing the competence of their staff members rather than the nature of their relationships. The perceived quality of the relationship is directly related to the senior pastor's perception of the staff member's level of competence. Senior pastors tend to value the professional skills and abilities of their staff members more highly than personality or relationship skills.

For example, Senior Pastor Todd Swanson said he appreciated working with his secretary, Laura, because she was fast, efficient, and always got the work done. He stressed that his relationship with Walt, the lay professional, was good because Walt had a strong youth and education background, and a lot of experience with young people. While Todd said that he had an adversarial relationship with his associate Karee, he believed that their working relationship had potential because of her excellent skills. He rated each staff relationship on the basis of competence and skills, rather than on personal and relational strengths.

Senior Pastor Ed Mantig also talked about his staff relationships in terms of skills and abilities. For example, Ed described his relationship with his associate, Marie Reilly, by saying that she was an excellent colleague because he knew she would do a fine job on whatever she undertook. He said she was good with people, a fine preacher, and a very capable person. Ed remarked that he had always had good associate pastors, but none with Marie's ability. He made it clear that while he and Marie were not friends socially, and rarely saw each other outside of the context of church, they had the finest collegial relationship that he had experienced in over 35 years of ministry.

Ed described his staff relationship with Sheila, the youth and education director, and Jean, the secretary, similarly. He talked about Sheila's fine skills in teaching, relating with youth, and in developing stimulating programs. He discussed Jean's competence in dealing with deadlines, angry parishioners, and crisis situations. Again, when asked to discuss his staff relationships, Ed described the skills and abilities that he valued in his staff, rather than any personal qualities.

Complementary Skills

Senior pastors also value complementary skills among their staff members. They believe the quality of their staff relationships is enhanced when each member brings different skills to the staff. My research has found that diverse and complementary skills contribute to good staff relationships.

Senior pastors perceive staff relationships as "good" when they have a blend and a balance of complementary skills. Most senior pastors appreciate a diversity of skills among their staff members because the staff and ministry is enriched by different abilities, viewpoints, and personality styles.

Todd recognized that Karee had skills in areas that he did not. He perceived that Karee's leadership of the women's groups and social concerns group was better than his own, and appreciated her contributing in those areas.

Todd discussed how Laura's easygoing, relaxed way of doing work and relating to people balanced his driving, aggressive work and relationship styles. He also mentioned how Walt's patient, inquisitive, and creative style complemented his own impatient, quick-moving, and practical personality.

Ed stated that their staff was strong because of their complementary skills and abilities. When asked why he appreciated his staff, he described their diverse abilities. He felt that Jean was much more efficient and effective on the phone than the others were. She also had excellent practical, detail-oriented office skills that were a real asset to their staff.

Marie was talented and had excellent preaching and teaching skills. She was especially interested in the liturgical dimensions of worship, while Ed was more interested in preaching solid sermons and using the same liturgy every Sunday. She complemented Ed's interests quite well.

Ed reflected that Sheila had many strengths and skills which neither he nor the other staff members had. He particularly valued her interpersonal relationship and counseling skills, and her ability to make people feel at ease.

Senior pastors generally perceive their staff to be "good" when the skills of members complement and balance each other. Such a balance is best achieved when members have roles which are in keeping with their individual skills and abilities.

Senior pastors desire skills in their associates which are diverse yet complementary because a variety of skills adds strength to the staff and the ministry. Increasingly, church agencies are assisting staff members in identifying their particular areas of strength, so that complementary skills can be enhanced, and trust can be further developed.

Trust

Trust is imperative for a staff if their staff relationships are to be workable and satisfactory. Trust enables a staff to rely on each other to fulfill their respective areas of responsibility.

In my interviews and research with senior pastors, I never raised the issue of trust. Every senior pastor, however, brought it up, stressing the importance of trust among staff members. They all stated that staff relationships cannot be good if the staff members are unable to fully trust each other.

Ed said that he and Sheila spent her first year on the staff struggling with conflict. It took quite a while for them to begin trusting each other. Ed's trust in Sheila developed more slowly than it had with other staff members. Yet Ed knew it was worth the investment because he believed that the foundation of his working relationship with all of his staff was built on trust.

Todd agreed that staffs need to share the experience of mutual trust. He stated that his problem with Karee developed partially because he didn't trust her to do what he asked her to do.

Trust is an essential dimension of a staff relationship. Rather than desiring friendship with their staff members, senior pastors prefer knowing that they can trust their staff. Thus senior pastors value competence, complementary skills, and trustworthiness in their staff more than they value any other traits or qualities.

What Do Staff Members Value in Their Colleagues?

Respect and shared role responsibility are qualities valued by associates on church staffs. The majority of staff associates who describe the quality of their staff as good or excellent do so in comparison to staff relationships in other parishes, which they perceive to be far less satisfactory. Marie, in describing her situation, said, "After listening to some of my female colleagues, I feel very fortunate to be in the place where I am. I have heard some real horror stories. My staff relationships feel about as collegial as they can be."

Male staff members also tend to compare their staff relationships to staff relationships in other parishes. They often perceive that their staff relationships are the best they can be. Unlike the senior pastors, the perceptions of associates about other staffs affected how they ranked their own staff. They did not judge the quality of their staff relationships by assessing competence or abilities of the staff as the senior pastors did. Rather, they talked about the quality of their relationships in comparison to other staff relationships. In addition, shared responsibilities and respect for each other were important factors.

Shared Responsibilities

Associates often attribute their positive staff situations to the fact that they are given full responsibility for their own areas by the senior pastor. Conversely, associates who are unhappy often feel that the senior pastor is in control of all areas in the parish. They describe situations where they do all the planning for a particular project, then the senior pastor makes the final decisions and may change the entire project. Associates desire to be given areas of responsibility and to make decisions in these areas in the way that they deem best. They value being the leader for certain aspects of parish life. In that way, they feel they are sharing and contributing to the ministry of the parish.

Marie, Sheila, and Jean believed that their staff functions smoothly because each has full responsibility for some dimensions of the parish life. Marie described their working arrangements, "Our responsibilities are divided up so that we all know who's in charge of what. We all do pastoral calling and share in responsibility for weddings and funerals. Ed is in charge of administration, finances, stewardship, worship, and preaches half of the time. I'm in charge of social concerns, and preach the other half of the time. Sheila coordinates all of the youth and educational programming, and the women's groups. Jean coordinates the Emergency Food and Shelter program, puts together the newsletter, and does all the secretarial work. But there's flexibility. For example, I love liturgy and planning worship services. Technically, that's Ed's area, yet he's open to sharing that area with me and giving me some responsibility."

Jean added, "I appreciate the fact that I'm regarded as an equal. They don't just dump whatever they don't want to do on me; they see me as an integral part of the staff. I have my areas of responsibility and the rest of the staff has theirs. We are committed to working together."

Sheila summed it up, "That's the key. Ed is accountable for the entire staff. Yet he gives us responsibility and treats us as people who are capable of coordinating our own areas of responsibility without his assistance or guidance. That feels really good."

Staff Have Different Preferences

While all associates want to have some degree of authority in their areas of responsibility, the need for power and leadership and autonomy varies with each individual staff member. This difference was apparent at First Lutheran. Karee had less satisfaction with staff relationships than did Walt and Laura.

Walt, the lay professional, said, "Our staff relationships are fine, although I would like it better if Todd trusted me in the areas of ministry for which I'm supposed to be responsible. The fact that Todd often gets involved with the final decisions of major youth events doesn't really bother me, but I do get annoyed when he pokes around in the everyday youth planning. Sometimes Todd tells me that something won't work, and so I spend a fair amount of time tangling with him and challenging him to think more creatively."

Karee, who works as associate pastor, says her staff situation is barely tolerable because Todd insists on being in charge of everything. She says, "The things that we share—preaching, teaching adult classes, pastoral calling, weddings, and funerals—all that is fine. What I get so aggravated about is that he is in charge of everything—when we preach, what I do in the funerals, what I teach in the adult classes, which people I call on in the hospitals. I am supposedly in charge of education, but he is constantly telling me what to do. Sure, I do some things on my own, but I'd be hard-pressed to think of more than two or three things in the past month that I've done without his involvement. I want more leadership and more responsibility than I'm getting here."

Associates desire to have responsibilities that they are in charge of. Having their own areas in ministry significantly enhances positive feelings about themselves and their work, as well as their satisfaction with their working relationships. If more staff members were able to discuss their role expectations with each other, to arrive at a common understanding, more associates would be satisfied with their roles and the way responsibilities are shared. Once a staff agrees upon particular ways to share roles and responsibilities, associates have a better chance of developing respect for their senior pastor. A healthy respect for one's co-workers is very important in any working relationship.

Respect

To define respect is difficult, yet vital. Respect is the recognition that we are all part of a common humanity, all created by God, all of equal value and worth. At the same time, however, respect is the affirmation and acceptance of that which makes us unique. In the staff setting, respect takes on the added dimension of each individual's unique humanity in the light of Christ, who encompasses all of us. As people baptized into the love and forgiveness of Christ Jesus, staff members are called by God to relate with respect and appreciation for each other's worth. As faithful Christians, God empowers us in our quest to respect the basic dignity and beauty of all people.

Respect is considered to be a necessary ingredient in good relationships by the majority of senior pastors and associates. They see it as crucial not only for positive staff relationships, but also for maintaining open communication. Those who do not respect their co-workers usually rate their staff relationships poorly.

Most staff members claim that respect for their co-workers is one of the most significant issues in determining the quality of their relationship. Consider the following comments at First Lutheran concerning the importance of respect.

Walt says, "You have to genuinely care about and respect each other. If you can't respect and care about a co-worker, I'm not sure about the quality of the relationship."

Karee says, "I think what makes a good staff relationship is a common passion and mutual respect. It is crucial that I respect the people I work with. Todd and I have a common passion for our parishioners, but our relationship is in trouble because I can't respect him as a pastor."

According to Laura, "The most important thing in our relationships is that we are able to respect each other's talents and interests. We also respect each other's authority in particular areas of ministry and we respect each other as people."

Respect is viewed as enhancing the quality of staff relationships. When a staff can respect each other, they are free to be open and honest. Respect allows open sharing about conflict.

Marie reports, "I really have a very high regard for Ed. I respect him. I think he's a very fair person. If I have a reasonable suggestion, he listens to it. I appreciate that we have mutual respect for each other."

Sheila describes their relationship, "It was difficult at first because I didn't respect Ed and he didn't trust me. I have come to respect him and the relationship is now open and growing. We express disagreement and we have a way of working things out."

Personal Relationship not a Priority

Most associates do not believe that personal friendship with their senior pastors makes a difference in the quality of their staff relationships. They feel that respect is far more crucial than personal friendship. Although the majority of the staff members I interviewed believe that they work quite well with their colleagues and have "good" staff relationships, they do not consider themselves friends with their senior pastors. Because they view respect as the most crucial quality in their team relationships, the level of friendship was not even an issue. Only two male associates in my research wondered if there might be advantages to being "friends" and "best buddies."

For example, Jean says, "Our staff relationships are certainly cordial, good working relationships, but by the nature of the differences in our four personalities, I wouldn't call us friends. We all have a great deal of respect for each other and our ability to do ministry in our given specialties. We have a high level of trust with each other."

And Marie comments, "Professionally the relationships among our staff are excellent, and personally they are all right. We're quite different. Therefore, we're not good friends. We are supportive and respectful of each other. We don't have any interpersonal or other kinds of major problems. We work easily together."

Most staff members do not believe that staff relationships need to be friendships in order for them to work well together. A few staff members even wonder if friendships with their colleagues might be detrimental to their collegial relationships.

Walt says, "I wonder how many members of parish staffs are friends and whether that is helpful or somewhat of a problem. It would seem that if the staff were friends, there would be so many other relational things that might get in the way of being confrontational, forthright, and honest."

Whether one uses the term "friendship" to describe a working relationship depends, of course, on how it is defined. Some see friends as buddies or pals who can be relied upon to support the "team effort." Others see friendship as involving respect, trust and mutual understanding—key elements of an effective working relationship. However it is defined, it is clear from my research that the intimacy normally associated with friendship is not a necessary part of effective working relationships.[2]

Summary

Three crucial components that enhance staff relationships are: (1) your expectations for your own role and the roles of your co-workers; (2) your preferences for qualities desired in your co-workers and the characteristics they prefer for you; and (3) your ability to talk with each other about these issues openly and honestly. Thus, if you know what qualities are particularly appreciated by other staff members and you possess those qualities, you can engage in tasks and responsibilities that would complement not only your co-workers needs, but also utilize your own skills. If you particularly appreciate an associate who preaches well and is creative with liturgy, it is helpful for your associate to know this in order that he or she may use and develop these gifts and interests. Staff relationships are enhanced when senior pastors and associates share their role expectations and desired preferences with each other.

Having examined the importance of making covenants, knowing role expectations, and being aware of and discussing the qualities desired in co-workers, it is now appropriate to reflect on the relationship between your family of origin system and your work system. Chapters 4 and 5 will examine how staff members often re-create dimensions of their families of origin in their staff environments. Through looking at the rules, closeness/distance patterns, communication and conflict styles, and roles in your family of origin, your staff relationships can be enriched by new insights concerning the similarity between those patterns and roles and the characteristics of your staff relationships.

4
DISCOVERING FAMILY AND STAFF SIMILARITIES

Your family and your staff are both systems. A system is a group of people who interact as a functional whole. Members of the system do not exist in a vacuum, but rather function interdependently with one another. A system has its own set of rules, roles, power structure, forms of communication, and ways of dealing with conflict.[1]

You are quite likely a member of a family system that includes at least three generations—you, your parents, and your grandparents. As a member of this system, you receive family beliefs and stories, and experience the influence of roles, expectations, and rules that have been passed down through the generations. You carry the patterns of your family system with you into all aspects of your life, including your work. Thus, in your work environment, you re-create dimensions of your family.

My research found that most staff members related to their colleagues in the same way they related to their families of origin. Both family and staff systems are affected by particular rules, closeness/distance patterns, communication and conflict styles, and family and birth order roles.

Rules

Systems are rule-governed, and system members interact with each other in organized, repetitive, and predictable ways. Research by Don Jackson found that among the system members, rules determine behavior to a greater degree than individual needs, drives, or personality characteristics. All family systems have rules for dividing labor and power, and most of these rules are unwritten and covertly communicated.[2]

You can discover your own family rules by recalling taboos, the "dos" and "don'ts" that you were raised with, as well as the injunctions you received concerning your behavior. Any phrases that use the words "always," "never," "ought," and "should" may well be a part of your family's rules.

What were your family rules? Take a few minutes to think about the rules that you learned during your growing-up years. What were the "shoulds" and "oughts" that you learned should dictate your behavior if you were to be acceptable?

Senior Pastor Todd Swanson, Associate Pastor Karee Lange, Lay Professional Walt Jacobs, and Secretary Laura Gentry all brought strong rules and beliefs about appropriate behavior and values with them into their parish staff relationships. Their personalities, behaviors, and relationships can better be understood by looking at their rules and beliefs.

Todd's family rules included:
- Always work hard.
- Be punctual.
- Always be the best.
- Be perfect.
- People can't be trusted to fulfill their responsibilities.
- You are ultimately responsible for everybody and everything.
- Dedication and self-sacrifice are important to succeed.
- Always work at getting ahead and making a name for yourself.

Karee's family rules included:
- Be successful.
- Be the best possible.

- Always be busy.
- Be responsible.
- Cover up your feelings.
- Never trust others with your feelings.
- Always smile—Don't cry.
- Always be nice.
- Be productive.
- Women shouldn't get angry.
- If you can't say something nice, don't say anything at all.

Walt also brought rules in from his family of origin into the workplace, including these:
- Be flexible.
- Don't rock the boat.
- Feelings don't exist.
- Be responsible.
- Follow through on your commitments.
- Don't talk about the family with others.
- Be private about personal matters.
- Go with the flow rather than stand up for yourself.
- Think creatively.
- Have fun and enjoy life.

The rules in Laura's family consisted of:
- You are more important than anybody or anything else.
- You are okay if you're feminine and cute.
- Let others take care of you.
- Do what others want you to.
- Women can't be effective leaders.

Karee's family rules were similar to Todd's rules. Karee believed that she was acceptable only if she was "successful," "responsible," and the "best possible."

The similarities between Todd's and Karee's family rules were behind the need they both had to be in charge, to be seen as successful, and to be fully responsible for many aspects of their ministry. Todd and Karee's conflicts were, in part, related to the similarity of their family rules. In addition, Karee subscribed to other family rules which said that she must "never trust," "never cry," and "always be nice." Thus, Karee felt that she couldn't even talk about what she was feeling.

When Todd looked at his own family rules, he discovered that he grew up thinking that he would be worthwhile only if he was "better than his peers," and "perfect" in most of what he endeavored to do. Todd, in a moment of vulnerability, talked about how he did not think the staff or congregational members would like or respect him if he was an "average" pastor. As a result, Todd felt he needed to push himself to excel and to achieve in order to be acceptable. Because of the importance of succeeding and making a name for himself, Todd felt a strong need to be senior pastor.

Todd and Karee's family rules had become laws that were dictating their lives and their staff relationship with each other. They need to discuss their family rules (make them public and explicit) so that some of the power of the rules can be dissipated. They also need to reflect on how they can turn their strong rules into guidelines for their life. For example, being successful and responsible is not such a powerful expectation if it is a choice and if one's self-esteem and sense of self-worth are not completely connected to it.

Rules affect expectations, and the disparity of operative rules within a staff affects staff effectiveness. In addition to staff members talking with one another about their rules and reflecting on how to turn their rules into guidelines, it is helpful for staff members to consider how God works with their rules and expectations.

Look at your own rules and expectations. Are you able to live and adhere to those rules? Are you able to measure up to your expectations? How is God a part of your rules and expectations? Trying to measure up to rules and expectations can be similar to living under the law wherein we can never quite measure up to how we feel we "should" or "ought" to be. In his death and resurrection, Jesus came to free us from the law and to empower us to live faithfully in love and forgiveness with one another. In Christ Jesus, God gives us the power to transform rules into guidelines, and to live in the freedom, love, and forgiveness of Christ.

Closeness/Distance

Rules are but one part of how a family interacts. Another factor is the degree of closeness/distance that families have in dealing with each other. This, too, affects how a staff will interact.

Close family relationships are not better than distant family relationships in terms of a well-functioning staff. Rather, my research found that similar experiences between staff in terms of family of origin, whether close or distant, are more important in enabling them to relate easily and smoothly with one another. Of the well-functioning staffs in my study, half had close relationships in both family and staff and the other half experienced distance in both their family and staff relationships.

As you read about closeness/distance styles of various church staffs, think about your own family of origin. Was your family "close" or "distant"? Did you interact and talk much with your family members or were you all fairly private and uninvolved with each other?

If you are in a staff situation now, do you see any parallels between the way you interact with your family and the way you interact with your staff? If so, how are the closeness or distance levels similar in your family and your staff? If they are not similar, how are the levels of closeness and distance in your staff relationships different from your family relationships?

Let's take a look at our two church staffs to see how closeness/distance patterns affect their relationships.

Good Staff Relationships: Closeness in Families and Staffs

Ed Mantig, Marie Reilly, Sheila Simons, and Jean Townsend exemplify a staff who characterized both their families of origin and staff relationships as close. They had experienced close family relationships and desired and created a close staff relationship.

Ed described his family. "We had strong ties with each other. We spent a lot of time together and enjoyed being together. There was a lot of love and care."

Marie said, "It is hard for me to be separated from my family. I miss them. We are extremely close. I miss talking with them and seeing them on a regular basis."

Jean said, "We had a lot of times in our family that we enjoyed being together. There was a strong family feeling, and that might have something to do with why it's so important to me to have a strong, close relationship with the staff."

Sheila remarked that it is nice to be on a staff that is like her family in the way they care about each other, disagree and fight with each other, and have fun together.

Ed, Marie, Sheila, and Jean feel close to their families and described their staff relationship in similar ways. They have a good working relationship, like each other, enjoy being with each other, and feel very fortunate to work together.

Staffs with good relationships feel that the closeness of their family relationships has enabled them to interact with their colleagues in ways that promote closeness. They relate to each other much like they relate to their families. They enjoy doing things together socially in order to get to know each other. By getting to know each other outside of work, they re-create their close family relationships.

Good Staff Relationships: Distance in Families and Staffs

Todd Swanson and Walt Jacobs typify a good staff relationship, where both Todd and Walt perceived family and staff relationships as distant, yet well functioning. Walt said, "There's a large age difference between my siblings and me. We're not close and we don't have much in common. Our relationships were rather distant and we each went our own way, but we get along fine. That's actually similar to how Todd and I work together. We like each other, but we don't have much in common. Each of us does our own thing, but we work well together."

Todd said, "Growing up, the only time I really saw my family was around the dinner table. We had our own lives and didn't talk much together, but we always saw each other at dinner. We cared about each other, but weren't real close."

A well-functioning staff relationship does not have to be close. As is evident from the example of Todd and Walt, the distance in their staff relationship was comfortable for them and in keeping with the distant relational patterns they learned in their families of origin.

Troublesome Staff Relationships: Disparity in Closeness/Distance Patterns

Problems may arise in staff relationships when there are differing closeness/distance preferences. One-third of the staffs that I interviewed had at least one staff member with a close family of origin relationship and at least one staff member with a distant family of origin relationship. Three-fourths of these staffs where staff members differed in their family of origin relationships had poor staff relationships. Thus the important factor in good staff relationships seems to be similarity of experience rather than the experience itself.

While Todd, Walt, and Laura perceived their staff relationships to be good with one another, Todd described his relationship with Karee as adequate and Karee described her relationship with Todd as poor.

One difference among Todd, Walt, Laura, and Karee was family closeness. Todd, Walt, and Laura were all distant with their families growing up and preferred the same distant staff relationships. Karee grew up in a close family system and desired to be close with the staff. The other staff members were more private and less interested in personal sharing. As a result, Karee was frustrated in the level of closeness of the staff.

Todd described his family of origin relationships as "functional with a fair amount of competition, alienation, and anger being overtly present most of the time." Walt said that everybody in his family of origin "got along adequately, but nobody ever really talked with each other about anything besides the weather, jobs, and neighborhood facts." But Karee described her family of origin relationships as "close" and said that she had "a good relationship with everyone."

Karee was frustrated and angry about Todd's inability to listen to her and be personal with her. Karee stated that she wanted a closer relationship with Todd and was dissatisfied with his distant style. She preferred working with a person who could be open and close with her in their staff relationship. But Karee knew that her preference for close interpersonal relationships in her staff, similar to her family, was just one piece of her struggle with Todd and their staff relationship. Even though Walt and Laura were distant in their personal preferences, Karee felt they listened to her and cared about her. They didn't have nearly the amount of interpersonal conflict that Karee and Todd experienced.

Conflict Styles in Families of Origin and in Staff Relationships

The majority of staff members in my study learned conflict styles of either openness or avoidance in their families of origin and continued to practice those same styles in their staff relationships. As you reflect on the following conflict styles of church staffs, take the time to think about your own conflict style. How did you deal with conflict in your family of origin? If you are in a staff setting, how do you currently deal with conflict? Are you satisfied with your current conflict style? If not, are you open to challenging yourself to learn a new way of dealing with conflict?

Closed Conflict Style in Family and Staff

Slightly more than half of the senior pastors in my study (but relatively few associates) were conflict avoiders. They described their conflict style with their families of origin in ways which were similar to how they described their conflict style with their colleagues. Recurrent phrases were "avoided it," "didn't know people or parents ever argued," "still struggle with it," "learned to suppress it," and "submerged it."

Todd said, "I was raised to deal with conflict by avoiding it or submerging it. I have tried to deal with it differently, but I know I keep slipping back to the old patterns of responding."

Karee discussed how she was considered to be "bitchy" whenever she expressed negative feelings. So she always did whatever she could to avoid conflict, sometimes even lying to herself and to others about what she was really feeling. Karee said that she still struggles with being honest with herself about what she's really feeling, and that discussing her anger or hurt is still exceedingly difficult.

Open Conflict Style in Family and Staff

Nearly half of senior pastors and the majority of the associates believed that they deal with conflict openly in their staff relationships. They perceived the conflict styles in their families of origin to be honest, direct, and straightforward. The conflict style learned in their family of origin is the conflict style that they continued to use in their adult lives and in their staff relationships. Ed, Marie, Sheila, and Jean's staff relationships demonstrate this.

Ed said, "I wasn't much for stuffing it. I let people know how I feel, and don't keep anything inside."

Marie agreed, "We argued and debated and challenged each other in my family. While our staff doesn't have a lot of conflicts, I can think of many times when we've also argued and fought about different issues here at the parish."

Jean added, "Actually, there are a lot of similarities between how we deal with problems in our family and how I deal with problems here with Ed, Marie, and Sheila."

Sheila said, "I'm better tempered now than when I was a child. My family dealt with conflict openly, but as the youngest little girl, I was expected never to express conflict. My family was open, but there was a different standard of behavior expected for me."

Changing Learned Patterns

Are you a person who is interested in learning a new way of dealing with conflict situations? While it is difficult to change patterns of behavior that enabled us to survive when we were growing up in our families of origin, change is possible. As people of faith in Christ Jesus, God gives us the power to successfully change old patterns of behavior. God empowers us to have the wisdom to know what we need to change in our lives and when, and gives us the courage to face our fears of change and seek a more healthy, life-giving behavioral pattern.

Such change is seen in a few of the senior pastors and associates in my study who avoided conflict in their families of origin. While they were able to learn new ways of dealing with conflict in their adult lives, there was evidence of their former patterns of avoidance in their new style of conflict management in their staff relationships. An example of this is Sheila Simons, the youth and education director at First United Methodist Church. Sheila illustrates how we can begin the process of seeking to change our conflict styles.

Sheila's family taught her that "nice girls are always sweet and agreeable." She wanted to be liked and so she took on a placating role with her family and staff. After a few years of ministry, though, Sheila felt that her ministry, her leadership, and her staff relationships were suffering because she could not face herself or other people honestly. Sheila worked hard at being honest about her negative feelings such as hurt, anger, and disagreement, and has been able to start being more open with her staff.

Sheila said, "I know that some of my early ways of dealing with conflict are still with me, but I feel I've come a long way from how I was raised. I often face conflict head-on with Ed, Marie, and Jean, and let them know when something is bothering me concerning our relationships. It's been a long struggle, but I believe that generally I now deal with conflict in a much more open manner."

Summary

A marked carryover of rules, conflict, and closeness/distance styles is evident from family system to staff system. Discovering the similarities between our family and staff systems challenges us to better understand our family systems so that we can develop more satisfactory staff relationships. Seeking the power of Christ Jesus to face our own rules, ways we deal with conflict, and closeness/distance styles in our family and staff systems gives us the strength, wisdom, and courage to develop more effective working relationships as people of God.

As in Sheila's case, who and where we are in the family (our role) has an impact on how we relate. Chapter 5 will further examine similarities between family and staff systems by examining the importance of family and birth order roles in staff relationships.

5
DETERMINING YOUR FAMILY AND STAFF ROLES

Roles are expected behavior patterns that are socially defined and that are a part of a social position, such as in a family or staff environment.[1] Each family member has a role in the family by virtue of their gender, birth order, and the particular family system. Our particular social position within any given system is an important element for working effectively together in any relationship. These roles are maintained by the family or staff system as a means of keeping the system in a balanced state. Thus, if the person who has the role of peacemaker suddenly refuses to take on that role, and instead becomes the comic, the system is thrown off balance and into some type of struggle or crisis.

Your Family Roles

Think about the roles you had in your own family of origin. What were your particular roles? Write down the names of each of your family members and beside each name put down at least two words that describe their roles. Possible roles might include:

peacemaker	comic
responsible one	nurturer
communicator	disciplinarian
scapegoat	caretaker
problem-solver	emotion-bearer
troublemaker	parent
protector	secret-keeper
storyteller	religious one
initiator	"baby"
comforter	adventurer
black sheep	organizer
smart one	challenger
disorganized one	quiet one
shy one	assertive one
conservative	liberal
succeeder	"darling"
agitator	rebellious one

There are many others. All of us, though, took on particular roles in our family that served an important function for us in our survival.

The significance of family roles is seen in the staff at First Lutheran. In his family, Todd took on the role of being responsible and perfect in order to get his parents' approval and to be noticed in his family system. This role continues for Todd in his belief that he will not be noticed or approved of if he is not perfect and responsible for everything.

In addition to being very responsible, Karee's family role was to be the "little mother," the nurturer, and the caretaker. Her sense of importance and worth was directly related to whether she was able to nurture and care for people.

Walt's family role was the bright, humorous, and quiet one, while Laura's role was that of the feminine, "darling," and peacemaker. Walt and Laura worked well with each other and the other staff.

Todd and Karee's roles fit well with the other staff, but not with each other. Todd did not want to be nurtured and taken care of by Karee, and did not want to trust Karee with having full responsibility for any area of the parish. Karee did not want Todd to be responsible for her, and did not know how to relate to him since the role she usually took on (caretaker) did not work in her relationship with Todd. The difficulties between them were partially due to the difference in their roles and the difficulty they had in relating with each other.

If you are currently part of a staff system, what roles do you think your co-workers had in their families of origin? Ask your co-workers if they would be willing to discuss each other's roles in your staff and how the roles that each of you play influence your staff relationships. If the staff agrees to do it, have everyone write down each person's name and put down two or three words which describe their staff roles. Spend an hour as a staff discussing your family and staff roles. An open discussion of the roles that you played in your families of origin and the roles you currently play in your staff could be immensely helpful as you and your staff strive to work more effectively together.

Senior pastors often take on a parental role with their staff members. While there are many dimensions to the parental role, one dimension involves how parents view their children. As parents often feel more positive about their relationships with their children than the children themselves feel, so senior pastors often feel more favorable about their staff members than the staff members do about their senior pastors. For example, Todd wanted Karee to stay and felt that their relationship was adequate, while Karee felt that their relationship was abysmal. Like a 16-year-old unhappy with her parents, she took on a "rebellious" role and wanted to leave her "parent" as soon as possible.

Your Birth Order Role

An important part of your social position within the family sphere is your birth order. How relationships are experienced by people can be a direct result of their particular birth order. Birth order roles, like personality types and family roles, are used as a general way of better understanding how a family functions. This discussion of the influence of birth order is intended to be used as a guideline for looking at birth order in your own family, in your own church staff, and in the way you experience it in other personal and professional contexts.

Research reports that people's birth order influences the personality characteristics of 70–80% of the adult population.[2] Assessing birth order as one component in selecting new staff and in further developing staff relationships, has not often been considered, however. Lyle Schaller recommends that if all the criteria in staff selection have a combined value of 100 points, in three-fourths (75%) of the cases we should give birth order a weight of ten to twenty points. Because he recognizes that not all people fit into their particular birth order roles, he suggests that the other one-fourth (25%) of the cases be given a weight of about zero to five points.[3]

In general, first-, second-, middle-, and last-born children possess particular personal characteristics that are specifically related to their birth order.

First-born children are often responsible, achievement-oriented, serious, diligent, possessing high expectations of self and others, maternal/paternal, leaders, and authoritative.

Second-born children usually possess the opposite characteristics of the first-born. If the first-born possesses the above qualities, second-born children are often more artistic, sensitive, less highly structured toward achievement, and less likely to take on parenting roles with others.

Middle-born children tend to enjoy people and relate well with people. They are often pleasant, relaxed people who are diplomatic, flexible and able to adapt well to a variety of people and situations. As middle children they are used to adapting to others.

Last-born children are usually fun-loving, playful, humorous, relaxed, casual in life-style (dress, appearance, home) and goals, good workers when interested in the project or idea, and able to work in subordinate positions.[4]

Birth order research can also be applied to families with only one child. Only children often possess high self-esteem and, as noted by Walter Toman in *Family Constellation,* often want to be the center of attention and under the guidance and protection of older people or people in positions of authority. Only children often need the care of their colleagues and superiors, want to please them and fulfill their wishes, and desire to be supported and helped more than others.

Some family systems do not fit the general birth order patterns; others fit the patterns in different ways. For example, in some family systems, the oldest child is more like a second-born and the second-born takes on the characteristics of the oldest child.

Furthermore, whenever there is a gap of over five and a half years between children, the birth order roles begin all over again. For example, if Amy is 17 and her brothers are 10, 9, 8, and 2, Amy and the 2-year-old brother will usually take on the characteristics of only children. They may also assume dimensions of the oldest role for Amy and the youngest role for the 2-year-old. Because of the age differences, the three middle children become like a family within a family. The 10-year-old is an oldest child, the 9-year-old a middle child, and the 8-year-old is a youngest child.

The more children in a family system, the more clearly pronounced the birth order role is. The oldest in a family of six children takes on the oldest child birth order role much more strongly than an oldest child of two children.

Having mentioned these exceptions and qualifications, it is still instructive to look at the general implications of birth order roles. As you read about the impact of birth order on staff relationships, think about your own birth order. Given your age and the age of your siblings, where do you fit in your family constellation? Are you a second-born child who may have taken on the role of an oldest child? How would you describe your personal characteristics? Does your description match that of your birth order role? Consider also the birth order role of your staff members and assess together where you all fit in your family constellations. In thinking about what works well in your relationships and what has been more difficult, consider whether those issues could be related to your birth order roles. (Much of this discussion on birth order roles has been drawn from Walter Toman's *Family Constellation.*)

Same Birth Order Role in a Staff Creates Stress

My studies of staff relationships found that the most problems arise when two of the staff members are both oldest children. Male/female oldest children have a more difficult struggle together than male/male oldest children. This is exemplified in Todd and Karee's relationship with each other.

The second most difficult working relationship is when a staff is composed of at least two of the staff being youngest children. The associates in this combination discussed how the pastors did not "take charge" in leadership roles, sometimes did not take administrative responsibilities seriously, were too relaxed and casual, and generally seemed to work only on tasks that were interesting to them. Yet, the positive side of two youngest children working together is that they are cooperative, flexible, playful, nonthreatening to each other, noncompetitive, and if they are interested in most facets of ministry, highly responsible.

Staff of Two Oldest, Only Female, and Youngest Brother

Senior Pastor Todd Swanson and Associate Pastor Karee Lange were both the oldest of six children who were all close in age. Both had three younger brothers and two younger sisters. Secretary Laura Gentry was an only child and Lay Professional Walt Jacobs was the youngest of three boys.

Todd: Oldest Brother of Brothers. Todd is like other oldest brothers of primarily brothers in that he loves to lead and assume responsibility for other people. Todd fits the oldest brother pattern described by Walter Toman in that he seeks to take care of other people, sometimes even bosses them around, requires loyalty and trust from others, and thinks he knows what is best for others.[5] He is highly reliable, but sometimes is quite arrogant in his beliefs about his own superior knowledge and abilities. Todd can be tough and cruel in his leadership style. As many oldest brothers of primarily brothers, Todd is concerned and acts responsibly, but his other family or staff members often regard him as too strict and too controlling. Toman's research found that men in Todd's sibling position work better with men than with women and can develop relationships better with younger siblings than with older siblings. This suggests that it would be better for Todd to work with male associates or with women who were not oldest children.

Karee: Oldest Sister of Brothers. Unfortunately for Todd and Karee, Karee is an oldest sister of primarily brothers. As an oldest sister, Karee is independent, strong, and likes to appear superior and "above it all." She works best with men who are youngest or middle children who have an older sister, since then she may be able to treat such men as little boys. As Karee has discovered, it is very difficult for an older sister of brothers to work with an older brother of brothers because such relationships often experience fights and conflicts over leadership and control with neither eldest child being willing to budge.[6]

Todd and Karee's Role Struggle. While two oldest children of large families can work effectively together, it is often more difficult. Todd and Karee's role struggle is evident in the way they talk about their relationship with each other. Recall Todd and Karee's conversation during their weekly meeting in Chapter 1. Their statements to each other suggest that their conflicts relate to their roles as oldest children. Both of them wanted to be in charge and in primary leadership positions.

Todd's voice was raised when he said to Karee: "You cannot add any change to our worship. I don't care what you learned at seminary. I'm the senior pastor, I've been here 22 years, and I know better than you what's best for this congregation."

Karee responded with anger: "I've had enough. I'm an adult and a pastor with good ideas. You're treating me like an 11-year-old child. I'm just not going to work at a place where I can't do anything on my own."

Todd believed that he could work with Karee and *trust* her if she listened to him and allowed him to carry out his rightful responsibilities as senior pastor and thus the pastor in charge of all leadership. Karee believed that she could work with Todd and *respect* him if she could be fully in charge of one or more of the areas of responsibility and programming in the parish, and if he would refrain from telling her what she should be doing in those areas and how she should be doing it.

Laura: Female Only Child. As an only female child, Secretary Laura Gentry depends on older people to take care of her. While Laura would never verbalize it, she wants Todd and Walt to be like her father and Karee to be like her mother. She tries to achieve this by bending over backwards to do what they want. Laura's birth order type works best with older brothers and sisters because they often provide paternal/maternal nurturing, care, and appreciation that the only female child needs. She has excellent relationships with Todd and Karee and is like the glue that holds the staff together. Todd and Karee want to interact with other staff members as leaders and as parents, and Laura needs their understanding, sympathy, attention, and parenting.

Walt and Karee offer Laura the leadership, affection, and parental guidance that she needs, and are generally able to communicate well with her and work well together.

Walt: Youngest Brother of Brothers. Walt Jacobs, as the youngest brother of three boys, needs to be respected, appreciated and understood by others. He is highly responsible and is a good team player who likes the collegiality of the staff, but prefers not to be the leader. As a youngest brother, Walt often is creative, assertive, and courageous. He likes to challenge people who are stronger than he is and may come across as a person who is obstinate or ambitious. Yet he is not an aggressor or cynic, but is softhearted, kind, and quick to forgive. He enjoys life and does not think much about income or debts. He is generous, impulsive, somewhat unstructured, and prefers the creative rather than the routine.[7]

In his staff situation, Walt gets along quite well with both Todd and Karee. He is comfortable with Todd and Karee having the leadership and parental roles, and with them providing him with nurturing, caring, guidance, structure, and responsibility. Walt has an adequate relationship with Laura. He would prefer working with a secretary who was less like him and who would take care of him; yet they are able to deal openly with their similarities and so relate well together on the church staff.

Different Roles Are Best for Staffs

Staffs with the best working relationship are ones which are composed of members with different birth orders. The ideal situation is to work with people of the same gender and birth order as your siblings.

The best staff relationships in my study were composed of senior pastors who were oldest children of sisters, middle children, or youngest children working with staff who were composed of an oldest child, youngest child, middle child, and/or an only child. Other staff compositions did work quite well, too, but often involved more work and energy.

Oldest Brother, Youngest Sisters, and Middle Sister

Ed, Marie, Sheila, and Jean are an example of an effective birth order configuration. Ed is an oldest brother of sisters, Marie is a youngest sister of brothers, Sheila is a youngest sister of sisters, and Jean is a middle sister.

Ed: Oldest Brother of Sisters. As an oldest brother with younger sisters, Ed's birth order role is to appreciate women. Ed deeply values Marie, Sheila, and Jean and interacts with them with a great deal of warmth, empathy, and understanding. While he works fine with men, he works best with women who are youngest sisters of brothers or middle children. Ed has had good working relationships with colleagues who have been oldest children, but did not care for their parental and at times authoritarian approach. As is typical of oldest brothers of sisters, he has a very low-key approach to his leadership style that is quite collegial. He expects good quality work, but does not like being the one in charge or like other staff members acting like they are the ones in charge.

Marie: Youngest Sister of Brothers. Marie fits into Toman's description of the role of the youngest sister of brothers. She is feminine, cordial, sensitive, and tactful. She is loyal to her co-workers and a good colleague. She admits that she gets what she wants from men and is spoiled by men.

Marie, like a younger sister of brothers, knows what she wants and how to get it. She is very flexible about most professional matters. Marie's birth order type works best with oldest or middle brothers who have younger sisters, and least well with youngest brothers or sisters or only children. She had problems getting along with Sheila at first, and has to work intentionally at developing a good collegial relationship with her.

Sheila: Youngest Sister of Three Sisters. Sheila has one older sister who is three years older and one who is six years older. She also fits Toman's description of a youngest sister of sisters. As the younger sister, she loves change and excitement. Vivacious, impulsive, erratic, easy to challenge, attractive, moody, and capricious describe her birth order role well. She is easily influenced by others and her opinions can change quite rapidly, depending upon who has most recently spoken with her. Sheila does quite well at work if she receives praise and appreciation.

Sheila's birth order type works most effectively with an oldest brother of sisters, oldest sister of sisters, middle brother of sisters, or middle sister of sisters because they usually give her understanding, guidance, and support. If she had just worked with Marie, they might have had difficulties because youngest siblings usually cannot provide each other with enough leadership, care, and support. If Marie had been old enough to be her parent and willing to take on a parental role, Marie and Sheila would have had an even better relationship.

Jean: Middle Child.   As a middle child of five children, Jean was accustomed to being flexible with people, schedules, and situations. She got along well with all the staff partially because, as a middle child of five children, she was particularly used to adapting to other people's needs. As is typical of her birth order role, she is gregarious, outgoing, friendly, personable, and has excellent relationship skills. Middle children generally work well with all of the other birth order types.

There are many similarities in rules, distance/closeness preferences, conflict styles, and family and birth order roles between staff and family systems. The interaction of a staff is, after all, much like that of a family. Once the characteristics of the family system are understood, the dynamics of a staff relationship become more clearly understandable. Your personality type is closely related to the roles you play in your family and staff relationships. How different personality types can better understand each other and work more effectively together is explored in the next chapter.

6

UNDERSTANDING YOUR PERSONALITY

G od has created us as beautiful and unique creatures. Your personality type is probably different from the personality types of your co-workers. The reality is that most of us are different from each other in fairly substantive ways. Our dreams, desires, goals, visions, values, beliefs, interests, motives, and ways of problem-solving are often very different. Our ways of thinking, processing, and feeling are also at times quite different. Often we find ourselves judging and putting labels on those who operate differently than we do. Because their attitudes, thoughts, and actions are different from ours, we think they are somehow less than we are. Almost imperceptibly, we see ourselves as superior to those who do not have the same quality of relationship skills, logical thinking abilities, creative abilities, and so forth.

We catch ourselves doing this in a variety of ways. Ed is very satisfied with the staff with whom he works. Yet while he extols Marie's competence and skills, at the same time he wishes that she would interact with more personal warmth and empathy. While Marie is quite pleased to be working with a man of Ed's caliber, she also wishes that he would debate more with her about theoretical and theological ideas. Marie thinks Ed would be a better colleague if he had more of her personality traits (especially her logical, analytical perspective), and Ed thinks Marie would be a better colleague if she had more of his personality traits (empathy, friendliness and warmth).

Understanding Our Different Personalities

As you reflect on the qualities and personality of the various staff members with whom you work, the Myers-Briggs Type Indicator (MBTI) is a valuable resource which is available to enhance your understanding of each other's personality. Based on psychologist Carl Jung's theory of psychological types, the MBTI is an instrument that shows us how our personality types are different from one another, how all personality types are valuable rather than some types being better than others, and how we can learn new ways of relating with people based on the strengths and possible limitations of our particular personality types.

The MBTI is composed of four type preference scales. While taking the MBTI is helpful in determining your type, this chapter will examine the various MBTI types in such a way that will allow you to consider which aspect in each of the following four pairs of preferences might best describe you. The four pairs are extroversion/introversion (E/I), sensing/intuition (S/N), thinking/feeling (T/F), and judging/perceiving (J/P). You will probably find that you have qualities of both of the pairs of opposites (e.g., extroversion and introversion). While you do use both pairs of the opposites, the question is rather which of the pair you *prefer* using. As you think about your type, consider what your tendencies and preferences are rather than whether you are completely one way or another.

Extroversion vs. Introversion: Where Do You Get Your Energy?

If you are an extrovert (E), you receive your energy from your outer world. Extroverts (E) tend to be sociable, enjoy many relationships, and tend to be action-oriented.

If you are an introvert (I), you tend to receive your energy from your inner world of ideas. Introverts (I) are not necessarily shy or quiet; rather, they are reflective people who enjoy thinking about ideas and concepts. Introverts may like people as much or more than extroverts, but their energy is depleted when they spend a lot of time with people and replenished through private space for thinking and reflecting.

Do you believe that your preference is more toward extroversion (E) or introversion (I)? While no general population figures are available, a reasonable estimate seems to be that 70–75% indicate a preference for extroversion (E) and 25–30% indicate a preference for introversion.[1]

In the staff at First Lutheran, Todd, Karee, and Laura were all extroverts and Walt was the only introvert. While Todd, Karee, and Laura were energized by long conversations and frequent interaction with each other, Walt found his energy depleted by interacting so continually with people. Walt needed more private space for thinking, reflection, reading, and planning programs.

While Todd knew that Walt had different relational needs than he did, Todd still interpreted Walt's wanting to be alone as not wanting to be with him or the other staff. Todd *felt* that Walt did not like him. After taking and discussing the MBTI, Todd, Karee, and Laura realized that Walt's relational needs were quite different from their needs. Walt's preference to operate with a great deal more private space than any of them desired in their own lives was a statement about Walt and not a criticism of any of them.

Sensing vs. Intuition: How Do You Assess a Situation?

We all take in information about situations through either sensing (S) or intuition (N). Sensing people seek to discover what a situation is about through their senses—using their eyes, ears, noses, and mouths. Sensing people often are practical, fact-oriented, and grounded in reality.

People who show a preference for intuition (N) tend to assess a situation through paying attention to their hunches, imagination, and inner voices. Creative, innovative, and future-oriented, intuitive (N) people like to speculate and dream about new possibilities and envision how things could be improved upon.

As you reflect on your own personality traits, do you believe that your preferences lean more toward sensing (S) or toward intuition (N)? While the general population seems to be approximately 70–75% sensing and 25–30% intuition, church musicians, lay professionals, and clergy seem to be more likely to have the intuition (N) preference and secretaries and volunteer coordinators are more likely to have the sensing (S) preference.[2]

At First Lutheran, 75% of the staff prefer intuition (N) and 25% of the staff prefer sensing (S). Todd, Karee, and Walt use their intuition (N) preference for creatively imagining new possibilities, ideas, and solutions for various projects, programs, and pastoral care situations. Laura uses her sensing (S) preference in keenly observing specific details, asking for all of the practical information, and making an assessment based on the known, observable facts about a situation.

In staff meetings, Laura is at times extremely frustrated. In discussing how Vacation Bible School was going to be led the following summer, Laura wanted to gather the specific details and facts from the previous summer's experience and plan the practical dimensions of next summer's program. Todd, Karee, and Walt immediately got engaged in a fascinating discussion (their perspective) about how the Vacation Bible School could be a bridge between various churches in the community, and how they could involve many of the other church staffs in the envisioning of a new and innovative program for children in the summer.

Laura thought to herself, "This is ridiculous. Summer is four months away, and there's no way this can be realistically put together in that time. I know very well who would be responsible for putting together all their wonderful ideas and I'm not going to do all of that work. We need to plan concrete details for the program. This discussion is not going anywhere!"

This staff needs to discuss how their different preferences in the area of sensing (S) and intuition (N) affect their working relationship. Both preferences are important in their staff relationships, and they all could benefit from respecting and seeking to understand the person operating in the opposite fashion.

Walt, Karee, and Todd could benefit from recognizing that they need to utilize some sensing (S) skills if they are going to sell Laura and others on their ideas. They must assess and deal with the facts and details of their ideas in order for the staff as a whole to work on the ideas together.

Laura could benefit from allowing the staff members preferring intuition (N) a chance to be themselves. Rather than immediately dismissing their ideas as impossible, she needs to suggest to them her concerns and ask them how they would deal with those concerns. Thus the staff with both sensing (S) and intuition (N) preferences can effectively work together on developing innovative projects that are realistic and possible to achieve in a given time-frame.

Thinking vs. Feeling: How Do You Make Decisions?

We make decisions about a situation based either on our principles (thinking—T) or our personal values (feeling—F). Thinking people tend to make decisions in an impersonal, objective, logical manner. They assess their principles and analyze the situation, with a firm and critical view of the operating standards, policies, and regulations.

Feeling people tend to make decisions in a personal, subjective, and value-oriented manner. Rather than primarily making decisions in an analytical, logical, and objective fashion (T) principles, the feeling people make their decisions based on their thoughts about how people will be affected. Thus, feeling people tend to concentrate more on personal factors, social values, extenuating circumstances, and relational issues.

It is important to realize that people who make decisions based on their principles (T) are not unfeeling or compassionless, and that people who make decisions on the basis of their personal values (F) are not without principles, standards, and firmness. It is simply a matter of personal preference (which they trust more) in how people chose to make decisions, and what preferences they rely on the most (T or F), rather than a reflection on whether T people have feelings for people or whether F people have the ability to think logically.

Do you believe your preference is more toward thinking (T) or toward feeling (F)? In the general population it is estimated that 50% prefer thinking (T) and 50% prefer feeling (F). Furthermore, it is estimated that the general population tends to be split 60% T for men and 40% T for women, and about 60% F for women and 40% F for men.[3]

Todd, Karee, and Laura prefer making decisions on the basis of feeling (F), while Walt prefers making decisions on the basis of thinking (T). This difference among the staff generally works well as their different T/F preferences balance each other in their decision making. In their decision-making process, Todd, Karee, and Laura are guided by their subjective feelings and values, while Walt's decision-making process is guided by his objective thoughts and principles. Thus, Todd, Karee, and Laura help Walt to consider important personal, relational dimensions of situations in decision making, and Walt enables them to see the importance of also considering logical, objective factors in their decision making.

The MBTI has helped the staff to realize that Walt's objective way of making decisions does not mean that he is cold, impersonal, and without feeling. They now understand, however, that Walt is not as feeling-oriented as they are and they need to clearly let him know what their feelings are about various situations. Once Walt understands their feelings, he is better able to consider their feelings as he logically analyzes various situations. Thus the staff now understands that he cares about people and about them.

Walt has learned from the MBTI that he needs to let the staff know how he feels. He has found that discussions proceed much more effectively if he begins by focusing on their common understandings and agreements. Then they can see that he is interested in working with them and they are less prone to becoming defensive. In order to maintain good working relationships, Walt has come to understand that he needs to establish the personal relationships and harmony before he disagrees and debates about particular issues. Likewise, the staff has come to understand that they need to engage their thinking function and consider objective principles in a logical manner before they disagree about particular situations.

Judging vs. Perceiving:
How Do You Live in Your Outer World?

Judging (J) people use the "judging" process (not to be understood as judgmental!) of thinking or feeling (T or F) in choosing how to live their outer lives. They like to control, structure, plan, and order their personal and professional lives so that they have as few surprises as possible. Decisions, punctuality, closure, and planning ahead are vital to J people.

Perceiving (P) people use the "perceiving" process of their sensing or intuitive (S or N) preference in establishing how they live in their outer world. They prefer a more flexible, open-ended, spontaneous way of life. Perceiving (P) people like to gather more information and adapt to situations as needed, and often need the external pressure of deadlines.

Judging people could be viewed as people liking closure, while perceiving people could be viewed as people liking to remain open to new information and ideas. Nonetheless, the qualities of judging and perceiving can be attributed to *both* the J and the P personality types.

In the general population it is estimated that approximately 50% prefer judging (J) and 50% prefer perceiving (P).[4] As it turned out, Walt was a P and Todd, Karee, and Laura were all

J's. The MBTI helped the staff to realize that Walt was not lazy or irresponsible but rather that he preferred to work in a less structured, less planned, and more spontaneous manner. They also realized that they themselves could learn to be more flexible and open-ended about some matters, and that they all could learn from each other. The other staff members decided that Walt could set his own pace for his programming, and they would try not to expect him to plan ahead in the same way they do. Because of their J preference, Karee, Todd and Laura became aware of the need to try to be more flexible and adaptable.

If you have not taken the MBTI, I encourage you and your co-workers to take it in order to better understand yourselves as individuals and as a staff. There are several different forms of the MBTI that are equally valid. You might want to consider taking the brief form of the MBTI in order to save time and money. If you have taken this inventory, I recommend continuing to utilize it in furthering your staff relationships. Many pastoral counselors in denominational social service agencies and career development centers have the training to give and interpret the MBTI. The Association of Psychological Type (APT), Box 5099, Gainesville, FL 32602, may be able to assist you in locating a person trained in the MBTI in your area of the country. A staff consultation with someone trained in the interpretation of the MBTI could be quite useful as you and your staff seek to understand and further your working relationships with each other. In addition, you and your staff could benefit from reading an excellent book on the MBTI entitled *God's Gifted People* by Lutheran pastor and psychologist Gary Harbaugh.[5]

Understanding your personality type and your role within a system is an important element in building effective staff relationships. But there are other dynamics operating as well. In the remaining chapters we will look at the dynamics of self-esteem, power, sexuality, communication, and conflict. All have a bearing on how well a staff works together.

7

STRENGTHENING YOUR SELF-ESTEEM

S elf-esteem is how people perceive their own worth.[1] People's self-esteem is often determined by their perception of their competence, skills, and behavior. Because it is based on how those around them perceive their behavior or on how others interpret their behavior, people find that their sense of self-esteem fluctuates.

Self-worth, on the other hand, is a gift from God that we receive through grace alone—not because we earn God's love, but because of God's great love for us in Christ Jesus. Through Jesus' death and resurrection for us, God says to us: You are forgiven! You are loved! You are that worthy! You are that special! God gives us complete love and acceptance in Christ Jesus, and give us a constant positive self-worth.

Self-esteem impacts and determines behavior, and is a deciding factor in how people interact with one another.[2] As a result, self-esteem is closely related to satisfaction in parish staff relationships. Clergy and lay staff members, like all people, need to feel that they are effective, competent, and cared about in spite of their weaknesses and failings. Four primary sources of self-esteem are: (1) visible accomplishment of goals and expectations; (2) evidence of personal power and influence over events and people; (3) sense of being accepted, valued, and cared about; and (4) behavior that is consistent with personal values and beliefs.[3]

A good sense of self-esteem is something that most of us recognize as something that would positively affect our relationships with our friends, family, and co-workers. However, my study results suggest that good self-esteem and belief in one's self-worth are crucial for effective staff relationships. All the staff members who perceived that they had high self-esteem also had good staff relationships and all the staff members who perceived their self-esteem to be low also had poor staff relationships. The correlation between the level of self-esteem and the quality of staff ministry relationships was quite strong. Staff ministry relationships have a much higher chance of being successful or at least satisfactory if the staff members have high self-esteem. Let us look specifically at the staff members we have already met and see how their self-esteem enhances or diminishes their relationships.

High Self-Esteem Enhances Staff Relationships

Ed Mantig stated emphatically that he felt the self-esteem of his colleagues was far more important than any other factors. Ed talked about working with Marie, "We have an excellent relationship. I don't think that gender, age, or experience in ministry makes any difference. It's personality and how people perceive themselves. I like myself and believe that I'm a good pastor and a good man. I'm not an extrovert but I have peace and self-assurance, and feel positive about myself. I think that Marie perceives herself in positive ways and has a good acceptance of herself and good self-esteem."

Marie Reilly was typical of many associates. She perceived herself to have high self-esteem and perceived the working relationship to be good because she was given freedom for her own areas of responsibility.

Marie said, "I feel good about myself. I feel fortunate to be in a working relationship where I have a free hand to do what I want to do. I think I'm relatively effective with people. The people that I work with are people who work hard, and who like experimenting. That makes me feel good."

Ed, like many of the senior pastors interviewed, believed that his high self-esteem came from relationships and experiences in ministry rather than from sources within himself. Ed was clear that he was able to maintain good self-esteem because he interacted and worked with people who also had good self-esteem.

Ed stated, "My self-esteem comes from a sense of care and support flowing back and forth, from relating to the people and the staff here. Because Marie, Sheila, Jean, and I feel good about ourselves and about our work, we are able to be mutually supportive. That makes our staff situation ideal."

Low Self-Esteem Diminishes Staff Relationships

All senior pastors who perceived themselves as having low self-esteem also had poor staff relationships. They did not have confidence in themselves and struggled with communication, conflict, and gender issues. The associates who perceived that their self-esteem was low attributed it to poor communication and lack of personal and shared power in their staff relationships. The influence of low self-esteem on a staff relationship is seen in the following example.

Youth and Education Director Sheila Simons had difficulty the first few years of ministry at First United Methodist Church. She often wondered what she was doing in ministry because she believed that she did not have leadership ability. She was competent in pastoral calling and participating in events, but she felt very inadequate in program planning or in the decision-making process. She never made a decision without first checking it out with the other staff members. She always took a notebook with her so she could keep track of their ideas and learn how to better plan events, understand people, and lead more effectively. The few times she made her own decisions, she found herself changing her mind at least ten times before actually going ahead with the plans.

Sheila talked about her struggle to be a leader, "I've worked hard these last few years trying to develop my own internal sense of self-esteem. I was raised always looking outside myself for a sense of who I am. I was always looking to others for approval and recognition. I felt like I was less than everybody else. I didn't even know myself as a person, let alone as a professional. I didn't think I had anything to offer. When I looked within myself for strength, I just found a void. I was really lonely and empty, and decided that I had to find myself or I wasn't going to ever feel adequate as a person or as a youth and education director."

Sheila, who has been at First United Methodist for four years, appears to be a different person. She walks confidently, is dressed professionally, speaks up at meetings, makes decisions and stands by them, and interacts as a full member of the pastoral staff. Needless to say, Sheila's self-esteem and self-confidence have grown significantly. How did she do it?

Strengthening Your Self-Esteem

Your self-esteem consists of your feelings about your own skills and competence, which affect not only how you relate with people, but whether you have the confidence in your ability to accomplish what you want, plan, and expect to do. Sheila intuitively knew that her survival in the staff system was dependent on developing both her self-esteem and her self-confidence. You, like Sheila, can begin enhancing your own self-esteem. The process involves several steps:

1. Remember how much God loves you.
2. Examine yourself realistically.
3. Identify strengths.
4. Identify negative messages.

5. Understand your feelings.
6. Reframe negative messages.
7. Believe in God's power and in your own power.
8. Know and respond to your own needs.
9. Develop additional skills.
10. Set goals.
11. Take risks.
12. Live by God's grace.

Remember How Much God Loves You

Remind yourself of who you are in the eyes of God. Recall that God loves you so much that Jesus died and rose for you. In your baptism, God claims you as a person of God and promises to be with you always. Take time to daily reflect on God's promises of love, forgiveness, and abundant life for you. You are a person of God because of what God has done in and for you in Christ Jesus, not because of anything you have attempted to do. You are worthy and worthwhile because of God's gift of grace.

Examine Yourself Realistically

Reflect on your skills and abilities. What can you do and what are you unable to do? Some of your feelings about what you cannot do may be inaccurate. It may be that your emotions are operating under assumptions that are based on events and messages that you received over 25 years ago concerning who you are and what you can do.

What are the current realities concerning who you are and what you can do? What are your feelings about tasks you think you are unable to do? It is likely that you are far more competent and talented than you feel you are.

Look realistically at who you are as a person of God. What does Jesus' death and resurrection mean for you? Do you trust in God's promise that you are a priceless gift exactly as you are in the midst of whatever you are experiencing? As you examine yourself realistically as a person of God, reflect on what God has done for you in Christ and on what Jesus says about you. As a person of God, it is completely realistic to believe and trust in God's grace and promises: You are a beloved, forgiven, and holy person of God.

In looking at herself realistically, Sheila's temptation was to run into Ed, Marie, or Jean's offices and ask, "What do you think my skills are?" She did not feel equipped to discern what she was good at—the word "competent" felt completely foreign to her. She forced herself, however, to sit at her desk and examine her own abilities, as well as her feelings about what she thought she could and could not do.

She also made herself take the time to reflect realistically on who Jesus said she was as a person of faith in Christ. She thought about how Jesus' love and forgiveness for her was not contingent on her thoughts or behavior, but rather was God's gift of grace and love for her.

Examining yourself realistically means to assess, honestly, with God's strength, your strengths and growth areas as a person of God. The good news of Christ's love and forgiveness can give you the energy and power to face your weaknesses and "reframe" them in a more positive way. Both your strengths and growth areas must be fully recognized in order for you to strengthen your self-esteem.

Identify Strengths

While it is not easy to do, make time to intentionally reflect on your own strengths. Make a list of all of the positive qualities that you possess. What are your strengths emotionally, socially, spiritually, mentally, physically, and professionally? Remember, what you know about yourself is revealed to you in your relationships with others. Add to your list every day. Once you have assessed your own strengths, ask for feedback from those you know and trust. Remind yourself of your positive qualities rather than dwelling on negative inner messages about yourself. Talk to God about your strengths, and pray that God will guide you in identifying your positive qualities. Believe and trust that

God has made you a holy, forgiven person, and that you are a person of beauty and strength.

As you begin to identify your strengths, look to how Sheila assessed her own strengths. When Sheila first started making a list, she couldn't think of more than six things that she liked about herself. She had pledged to herself that she would think of at least 25 positive attributes and so she decided to think of at least two words to describe herself for each letter of the alphabet. She began with "A," and thought of "affectionate," then her mind drew a blank. "Awful"—no, that's not positive! "Alluring"—well, not really. "Adorable"—not really true. She decided to get a dictionary and peruse each letter until she found two positive words that described her.

Sheila also decided to pray for God's help in discerning her strengths and gifts. As she prayed, she realized that her struggle to identify her strengths would have been easier if she had thought of praying for God's power initially. As she prayed, however, she found strength and courage in God's presence with her as she talked with God about who she was and what her gifts were and as she listened quietly to God speaking within her spirit. Reflecting quietly in God's presence and power was renewing for Sheila as she assessed her own strengths as a person of God.

Identify Negative Messages

Reflect on the negative messages you received about yourself from the people around you when you were growing up. Your messages might include:
- You're unacceptable when you're angry (never be angry).
- You won't be likeable if you say anything negative (always be positive).
- It is wrong to talk about personal matters with other people (you're not important).
- Don't say anything controversial (don't be real and genuine with others).

Write down some of the negative messages you were taught when you were young. Do these messages accurately describe who you are and what you are able to do today? What are some new negative messages that you give to yourself?

Make a list of at least five of the negative messages that you still give yourself. Where did you learn them? Who gave you these messages? What keeps you believing these negative messages?

Sheila did not have a problem thinking of five negative messages. In fact, she wrote down seven:

- Your sister is the smart one in the family.
- You can't do anything well.
- You are too scatterbrained.
- You are too feminine to be capable or smart.
- You don't have the ability to make good grades.
- Always let responsible people make decisions.
- You don't have what it takes to be a leader.

Sheila realized that her parents and siblings wanted her to be helpless so they could take care of her and she could be their "little darling girl." It was Sheila's decision whether or not to continue to accept that she was not able to be decisive, smart, clearheaded, or capable. Yet she could not do this without God's power and grace. As a faithful, forgiven person of God, Sheila felt empowered and led by Christ's love to believe and trust more in God's deep love for her as a person of worth and value.

Understand Your Feelings

Before negative messages can be dealt with, they must be faced, that is, felt on an emotional level. Some of the negative messages you received were so painful that you had to deny and bury those feelings in order to survive. The pain of one of your parents saying, "You are only OK if you get A's,"—that is, "be perfect," must be felt so that your hurt can be expressed.

Getting in touch with your feelings involves asking questions, such as, "How am I feeling about this message? Why is this message emotionally difficult for me? How have I dealt with this feeling before? What can I do about this feeling now? What does God say to me about this message? Who does God in Christ Jesus say I am?" To truly face our feelings is to be vulnerable with ourselves and with God. Through God's grace, Christ is with us and empowers us in such honest reflection so that we will know increased growth and life through confronting our feelings so directly.

As Sheila allowed herself to recognize her feelings, she began to realize that she was angry about having had to be a sweet, nice, and cute little girl that never had negative feelings. Sheila was raised to "stuff" her negative feelings and to either cry, withdraw, or giggle when she felt angry. She decided to identify her negative feelings and learn how to communicate those feelings to her family and colleagues. She realized that when she was upset with Ed, she usually cried. While she was raised to think that people would not like her if she was angry, she decided that "stuffing" her feelings was destructive for herself and her relationships. She realized that she had to stop hiding her genuine self from others, from herself, and from God, and start believing that people would like her even when she was angry.

She further decided that she needed to listen more closely to Jesus' words about who she was as a person of God. She reminded herself of God's grace: that God saw her as she was— a forgiven, loved, worthwhile, beautiful person in Christ Jesus. Thus, she knew she could express her true feelings with people because she was completely acceptable and lovable as a person of God, and God could give her the power and strength to be more open with people about her genuine feelings. To "stuff" her feelings was not to trust fully in God's presence and power in her life.

The next time she was crying and withdrawing from Ed, she asked God and herself, "What am I really feeling?" Through God's power, she slowly realized that she was hurt and angry that Ed hadn't given her support when she shared with him a situation concerning an angry parent. Now that she understood her feelings, she wasn't sure if she had the courage to talk to Ed. Because she knew that needed to be the next step, she prayed that God would grant her the courage and strength to talk honestly with Ed.

Reframe Negative Messages

To reframe a negative message is to change the message into one which is a more positive way of viewing yourself. Your negative messages must be faced head-on and reframed in order for those messages to lose their power. Otherwise the negative messages that you carry will keep affecting your thoughts, feelings, and behavior in ways that take away from all you can be.

Sheila could only reframe the negative messages if she believed she had the potential to behave differently from the way in which she had been raised to behave. She needed to listen to God's action in Christ Jesus which clearly states she is a person of infinite worth. She also needed to believe in God's power as well as in her own power and ability to change. Through God's grace and power, she knew she could reframe the negative messages about her personal qualities and professional abilities which had been ingrained since her childhood.

To reframe your negative messages, take another piece of paper and write down one of your negative messages. Now write a new message that is more positive. Say exactly why the old, negative message is not true any longer and give evidence of how the new, positive message is valid in your life today.

Sheila shows us how to do this. First, she identified one of her learned negative messages. "You are likable only if you are always nice, sweet, and cute. You won't be liked if you express negative feelings such as anger." Second, she pushed herself to understand her feelings about this message, and realized that she was angry about this message and did not like having her behavior so confined. Third, she assessed whether this message still applied to her today. She believed that this message worked for her while she was growing up, but in her current life situation it was destructive to her and to her relationships. Fourth, she reframed it by writing a new message.

"I am likeable when I am nice, sweet, and cute if that is how I really feel. I am also likeable when I express my genuine feelings—positive and negative—to others. I am not likeable when I hide my negative feelings from myself and from others."

Another example is found in a negative message Sheila always heard from her parents and older brother and sister. "You can't do anything well." In reframing this negative message, Sheila wrote, "I can do many things well. I can speak in front of large groups. I can communicate with care and empathy. I can relate to many types of people. I can lead Bible studies and discussions."

Recognize and Believe in God's Power and in Your Own Power

By believing and trusting in God's tansforming power, Sheila was able to begin believing that God in Christ Jesus could empower her to develop confidence in who she was as a competent, gifted, adult member of a staff relationship. Sheila began living as though Christ did die and rise for her and for all people. This meant that she embraced the gospel message of God's complete and unconditional acceptance, love, and forgiveness for her and began trusting that God in Christ Jesus truly was calling her, empowering her, and with her as she struggled to grow and develop as a person and church professional.

By recognizing her own power given to her by Christ through the Holy Spirit, Sheila was able to assess whether the negative messages she learned from her family about herself were true. It was up to Sheila to decide whether she wanted to keep believing old messages that took away from her potential. She recognized that God believed she was a priceless gift and that she was truly created in God's image. As a faithful person of God, she had a responsibility to herself and to God. Through God's grace and power, Sheila could assess who she was and what she could do.

Only by recognizing that you alone have the right to evaluate your own personality and ability can you begin to let go of other people's ideas concerning your personal attributes and skills. Each of you, like Sheila, has the capability and personal power to make decisions concerning who you are, who you want to be, and what your areas of competence are. While others may want to evaluate you and your skills, only you know yourself and only you have the power in Christ Jesus to make decisions about who are you and what you can do.

Your self-esteem and self-confidence will be like a roller coaster, in a constant state of flux, if you are relying on praise and recognition from other people to help you feel good about yourself. By listening to what God says about you and by being in touch with your own feelings and aware of your own skills, you are able to be in charge of your own self-esteem. Thus you are able to claim your own personal power in Christ Jesus and depend on God and yourself for feeling positive about yourself. With your self-esteem firmly established, compliments from others will confirm and affirm what you already know about yourself. While compliments and affirmations feel good, such praise will not be essential to keep your self-esteem high.

Constructive criticism is also important feedback for strengthening your self-esteem. In the context of the faithful, forgiven community, we strengthen our self-esteem when we encourage our co-workers to give us positive and negative feedback. In addition, we need to listen attentively to the constructive criticism that we receive from those who know us in our communities. Through seeking and listening to the negative as well as the positive feedback, we enhance our self-esteem.

Know and Respond to Your Own Needs

In Christ Jesus, you have the power to make intentional choices about who you are and how you live. You can actively decide upon your style of communication, your relationships, and your life. This involves knowing your own needs and desires, and assessing how these personal and professional aspirations can be reached. This also involves praying and trusting that God will empower you to better assess and respond to your own needs so that you can be a more faithful servant in ministry for your sake, for your staff's sake, and for the sake of the people whom you serve.

As a faithful person of God, what are your needs and desires? Your self-esteem is enhanced if you are able to understand and respond to your needs from a personal, professional, social, intellectual, spiritual, and physical perspective. As you reflect on your needs and desires as a person of God, seek God's wisdom, discernment, and power.

On a personal level, what do you want for yourself? Professionally, what are your aspirations and goals? What are your desires in terms of your social life? Intellectually, what are your needs? What are your desires for yourself on a physical level? How do you want your spiritual life to be?

After evaluating your needs and wants, it is important to reflect on the process by which you will achieve these desires. In so doing, your self-esteem and self-confidence will be strengthened.

When Sheila reflected on her own needs, she discovered that she had a need to be a competent and respected youth and education director. She did not want to be just cute. She also wanted to be respected as a faithful leader of the gospel who possessed intelligence and wisdom. She wanted to be viewed as a person who added maturity and depth to discussions and church leadership. Sheila determined that she needed to act more like she wanted others to perceive her and that God could empower her to become such a person. She decided that she would begin asking intelligent questions and contributing thoughtful comments at the various meetings she attended. She would be intentional about acting in a mature and responsible manner. And she would think about her comments before impulsively responding to whatever triggered her interest and fancy. Sheila had a picture in her mind of how she wanted to be perceived, and she worked hard at developing behavior which was wise, intelligent, mature, and faithful to the gospel.

Develop Additional Skills

In order to accept that she was capable, Sheila needed to trust that God was continually working within her and empowering her, and she needed to increase her competencies as well as acknowledge her existing abilities.

In terms of personal skills, Sheila felt she would be more faithful to the gospel and to her calling as a person in ministry if she became more independent and autonomous. She struggled with being indecisive and easily influenced by others, and wanted to develop the internal strength to make her own decisions and be her own person.

On a professional level, Sheila wanted to develop the skills to teach adults. There was a university in the area which offered master's level courses on effective adult education. Sheila decided to approach the church council for permission to take one course a semester in this field.

Assessing the personal and professional areas in which you need to further yourself as a person of God is crucial to the development of healthy self-esteem. Believing that you are loved and accepted by God as you are, liking who you are, and believing that you have valuable skills and expertise increases your own confidence in yourself. Thus you know that God has given you personal power, made you a person of worth, and that God in Christ Jesus enables you to be a competent professional. This confidence is reflected in all your relationships, whether they be at work, at home, at church, or at play.

Set Goals

Changes in your personal attributes and abilities do not magically occur even though you wish they would. Through the guidance and power of the Holy Spirit, you need to set goals that are precise, realistic, and measurable. Be specific about what your goals are and how you are going to attain them. Make sure your goals are realistic ones that can be accomplished. Decide how you will evaluate whether your goals have been reached.

What do you want to change in your life? List at least five things you want to change. These changes might include beginning an exercise program, learning to communicate negative feelings, changing your conflict style, developing a more intentional prayer life, increasing personal time with family/spouse/significant others, and modifying smoking, eating, drinking, working, and recreation habits.

When are you going to make these changes? If you want to start exercising on a regular basis, can you start tomorrow or next Monday? Which days and at what times are you going to exercise? Be specific.

How are you going to insure that you make these changes? If you are going to start exercising tomorrow, will you join a YMCA/YWCA, a health club, or do it on your own? Will you walk a mile a day, swim a quarter mile, do aerobics for twenty minutes, or exercise on a bike? Write down the type of exercise that you'll be doing.

What factors will contribute to your ability to make these changes and reach your goals? Pray and reflect thoughtfully and write down these supporting factors. If one of your changes is increased exercise and you've decided to swim one-half mile three days a week at the YMCA/YWCA, what will help you to achieve this goal? Swimming with a friend, swimming on your lunch hour or at the beginning or end of your working day, thinking sermons or programs through as you swim, or having your swim time always blocked out of your schedule?

What factors might get in the way of reaching your goal of swimming one-half mile three days a week? If you are aware of these roadblocks, you can plan your swimming with these in mind. For example, if your schedule is always full and crisis situations happen constantly, perhaps you need to swim prior to going to your office or have a set time in the afternoon or evening that is your time to swim.

One of Sheila's goals was to relate with Ed in an adult–adult relationship. While she wanted to improve her relationships with the entire staff, Sheila decided it would be easier to concentrate on one particular staff member. Because she trusted him, Sheila chose Ed.

For Sheila, an adult-adult relationship meant that she would be less impulsive, less erratic, less easily influenced by his opinions, and less in need of his praise, recognition, and support. In her new relationship with him, she prayed and set goals wherein they could become colleagues sharing perspectives, feelings, and ideas with one another. With God's grace, they would be able to work more as a team together and would offer wisdom, advice, and support to each other in a mutually interdependent way. This would be different from their current way of functioning—Ed always giving advice, guidance, and praise, and Sheila always receiving his suggestions and affirmations. It was a goal which could be achieved, but one which would take several months to accomplish. Sheila decided to make it a three month renewable goal that would be measured by self-evaluation in a journal. She made the commitment to herself to write in her journal every night about the specifics of her interactions with Ed. She would particularly note ways in which she was more adult-like in her interactions with Ed, what she did that was more mature and adult-like, areas in which she slipped up and how to correct that, and any feedback Ed gave her on this subject.

She decided that an adult–adult relationship with Ed meant that she needed to:

- stop asking his opinion on everything she did;
- ask his advice less frequently on aspects of her youth and educational ministry programs;
- ask for at least an hour to reflect on changes that Ed suggested in her areas of ministry;
- reflect on Ed's opinions on any subject before responding;
- discuss topics on which she gave her opinion;
- listen to Ed's opinions without immediately changing her own stance on the issue;
- look to herself for recognition on her accomplishments; and
- not expect Ed to affirm and support her.

She knew that putting these goals into practice would take a great deal of time and energy, but with God's power, an increased sense of high self-esteem, and the support of the staff, Sheila was hopeful that she could accomplish them.

Take Risks

To risk is to encourage change. Your life and staff relationships can change for the better if you risk trying new ways of thinking, feeling, and acting. Risk-taking is often frightening because it means venturing out into the unknown. Many people stay in unhappy situations because what is known is easier and less scary than facing new situations. If you don't risk, however, little change is possible and you will not grow to your full potential in Christ Jesus. Risk-taking is about growth and seeking the best. To risk is to trust God, trust yourself, and increase your self-esteem.

Admittedly, Sheila recognized that trying to establish an adult-adult relationship with Ed was a risk. She had to continue working with him and didn't want to ruin the relationship they had, despite its faults. Plus, she didn't really know if she could be the leader she wanted to be and was scared about running the youth and education programs on her own. Perhaps, if the truth were known, it would be that Ed was the "behind-the-scenes leader" in almost all of Sheila's activities. She didn't do anything without checking with him. "Perhaps," she thought to herself, "this is too big of a goal to begin with and too big of a risk. I'm risking my relationship with the person I work with most and am risking my job." But Sheila also knew that she needed to make this kind of change and believed that God would show her the way. She could take a little bit at a time, with the primary goal being to develop a more adult and healthy relationship.

Sheila decided to "reframe" her fear of this goal. Instead of seeing it as a potential losing situation, she declared to herself that no matter what, she would win. First, she would develop new skills for relating in an adult fashion with other people, even if it didn't work with Ed. She told herself that she had nothing to lose with Ed because the relationship was not particularly satisfactory to either of them as it was, and it really couldn't get much worse. Second, there was almost no way she could ruin her job. If the worst happened and she had a month of unsuccessful and disastrous programs, she would allow herself to consult with other youth and education directors in the area. And finally, Sheila told herself that it was far more likely she would learn how to be a more effective leader, a more competent youth and education director, and a more decisive and skilled church professional.

Thus Sheila "reframed" the risks and looked at what she would gain from taking the potential risks. She decided that the gains far outweighed the losses.

To not take risks is to allow your fears and negative messages about yourself to take over your life. Risk-taking is about opening yourself up to new opportunities to grow and develop and thus is about increasing your confidence in yourself. When you assess the new ways in which you would like to develop, you can either talk yourself out of taking risks by concentrating on the negative or you can "reframe" the negative, focus on the positive, and look at the risks as an opportunity for growth and new life for yourself. To risk is to face your fears and negative feelings head-on, to trust in God's presence, guidance, and power, to believe in yourself and your own personal power, and to have confidence in yourself as a faithful, forgiven person of God.

To risk is to be yourself and be true to your own feelings, thoughts, and desires. It is to be authentic with yourself and with the people around you. While risk-taking is not easy, it is imperative for your own personal and professional growth and for your self-esteem. When done in the context of the covenant community of a Christ-centered staff, you are empowered to risk, trusting that you are not alone.

Live by God's Grace

Developing your self-esteem, assessing your needs, setting goals, and taking risks is about living by God's grace. It is only through God's grace—the unconditional love and forgiveness of Christ Jesus for you in the midst of whatever you are experiencing—that you are able to know Christ's presence, love, and acceptance of you as a person of worth, and Christ's power that enables you to live as a faithful, grace-filled, and forgiven person of God. Staff relationships are enhanced when you are able to trust in God's promises of love, forgiveness, and power, and let God in Christ Jesus nurture and strengthen your confidence in yourself as a person of God.

Closely related to strengthening self-esteem, living by God's grace, and risking is the recognition and use of power in staff relationships. Chapter 8 explores how to recognize and strengthen your personal power in Christ Jesus.

8
RECOGNIZING
YOUR
POWER

Power is central to our personal and professional relation-ships. Often viewed negatively by people in the church, power is a very present reality in any human situation. As with any part of God's good creation, we may use it creatively or we may abuse it. While "power" has many different meanings, it is defined here in the personal sense, as the ability to control one's own life without dominating or controlling others. People use power in covert and overt ways. Generally relationships function best if power is expressed in overt, clear, and direct ways. When power is used in covert ways, people tend to act in secretive, hidden ways. Thus power becomes abusive and a barrier to effective, healthy relationships.

Your Power Style

How we respond to power and how we use power impacts our relationships at work and at home. Some of us fear personal power and try to pretend that it does not exist. We deny that we are capable of making decisions; we accept tasks and re-sponsibilities that we do not enjoy; we do not let family, friends, and employers know how we really feel about anything. Self-esteem is diminished when we give up or fail to acknowledge our personal power—the power we have to impact our own lives, and to influence or empower others without controlling them.

Some of us have a healthy respect for our own power. We speak up for our own needs and desires, taking into consideration the needs and desires of others without attempting to control them. We say what we actually think and feel instead of what we "should" think and feel. We assert our thoughts and opinions, rather than blindly accepting how others say something should be. Our self-esteem is enhanced when we seek to influence and control our own lives, rather than allow others to control and have power over us.

When the relationships among staff members are examined, there emerges a clear correlation between the level of self-esteem and the use of power. Low self-esteem corresponds to expressing power in covert ways, or to giving up personal power. High self-esteem relates to controlling one's own life as well as to using power to empower others. In my research, church staffs with positive self-esteem functioned much better in terms of sharing power and leadership. Church staff members who identified themselves as having high self-esteem demonstrated more mutuality in their decision making, and employed a more collegial leadership style than did staff members with low self-esteem. Church staffs who shared power and leadership not only made decisions through group consensus, but acted as resources for each other. This is quite different from the church staffs with low self-esteem where usually one person was in charge of making most of the decisions and directing the staff in all their tasks.

Power as a Tool for Staff Relationships

Church staffs who possess high self-esteem view power as an effective tool for two distinct functions: (1) influencing and persuading; and (2) empowering others.

Influencing and Persuading

Some people define power as the ability to influence and persuade. Their role involves getting another person to think or act in a way which is new or different for them. People with persuasive power voice their thoughts and opinions. They do not control the decisions of others, but they can influence the decisions of others by providing additional insight and information so that more aspects of a situation can be considered. The degree to which a person is able to influence or persuade is primarily related to status, knowledge, and self-esteem.

Status involves the person's role as well as the person's gender. Except for co-pastors, staff members usually possess different roles and statuses. In the eyes of the congregation and as evidenced by salaries, ordained staff usually have higher status than lay staff. Senior pastors have higher status than assistant or associate pastors; lay professionals have higher status than secretaries. Male associates often have more power in congregations than female associates.

Yet the gospel message is clear: All people are called to be equal in Christ Jesus. All of us need to be consciously aware of our own classism and sexism, and work intentionally toward staff and parish relationships that are more truly partnerships as faithful, forgiven people in Christ Jesus.

Letty Russell says it clearly, "The persons find their focus of relationship in Jesus Christ, and their commitment to Christ and to the task of service at hand makes them equal members of the partnership. This equality and mutuality of support must be recognized by all the partners so that those who have less 'status' can claim for themselves their own self-identity and worth."[1]

Knowledge is expertise in a particular area. In a discussion on finances, we pay more attention to the person who has the background, credentials, and experience in financial matters. In determining how to best select educational programming materials, we generally look to the staff person who has had experience or training in education. If, however, both the senior pastor and youth director have experience and expertise in educational programming, it is likely that the senior pastor will have greater influence in the decision-making process. The person with the greater influence is the person with the status and knowledge. So, if two people display the same relative level of expertise, most of us will look to the person with the higher status for guidance. If status is accorded because of level of accountability, that may be appropriate. If status is accorded because of gender, we must face our own sexism and look at ways that we can move beyond it.

A person's ability to persuade and influence is also dependent upon his or her level of self-esteem, which must be considered in conjunction with status and knowledge. If a female associate has a high level of self-confidence and knowledge, and does not buy into the belief that she has a lower status, she can overcome the stigma of having a lower status, and be quite persuasive and influential.

Almost half of the senior pastors and one-fourth of the associates used power to persuade and to influence. They viewed personal power as a way of influencing people without coercing them.

Senior Pastor Ed Mantig views power in terms of his ability to persuade people. He feels that he accomplishes this through language, ideas, and theology. His style of leadership in committee meetings is to suggest alternatives or articulate questions. This allows people to reflect on his ideas in such a way that ultimately they make their own decisions. He does not control them or their decision-making processes.

Many of the male senior pastors and male associates talked about influencing rather than coercing people. Since most males talked about persuading, it is conceivable that their ability to persuade is partially related to the status accorded the male gender. They perceived that the pastoral office (thus their role status) gives them a great deal of ability to influence. They believed that power is the ability to move people in the direction which they think is best, while still allowing the people the freedom to make their own decisions and go in a different direction.

Empowering Others

Many of the women associates stated repeatedly that power is to be used for enabling and empowering others. A sense of power as empowering others is quite different from power as influencing or persuading others. While people who use power to influence others usually are seeking to maintain or increase their own personal power base, people who seek to empower others are attempting to establish power in another person.

Empowering others is twofold: (1) enabling others to know their power without giving up your power; and (2) equipping others to know their gifts, skills, and full potential.

People who seek to empower others do not give up their own personal power, but rather enable others to know their own power. While many still believe it, it *is* a *myth* that there is only a certain amount of power to go around and if you do not grab it, you will not have any power. Such an attitude is based on a scarcity model of power—one which sees power as limited and finite. An increasing number of people in ministry view power as limitless and believe that power regenerates and expands when it is shared. Power increases when it is shared.[2]

The associate at First United Methodist, Marie Reilly, believes that empowering others is directly related to the good news of Christ Jesus who empowers us to be people who exercise our own power, freely and creatively. Rather than feeling that the staff should have all the power, Marie feels more comfortable when many of the staff share their power, helping others realize their own power. Marie believes that empowering people to claim their own personal power enables more effective ministry to occur.

Another component of empowering others is enabling them to better know their own strengths, abilities, and potential. Youth and Education Director Sheila Simons described her commitment to empowering others by saying that she believes that everybody has power. She also contends that her own power is expanded when she helps other people gain a sense of their power, worth, and abilities. She enjoys being in an empowering position, rather than in a position where she tells others exactly what to do.

Empowering is also about encouraging people to further develop their gifts, skills and potential as people of God. Associate Pastor Karee Lange describes her leadership style as empowering, where her job is to use her power to help people claim the power that Christ Jesus gives them. She sees it as ideal if the church can function whether she is there or not, except for the official things she has to do. In Karee's mind, the more she can empower the people to run the church, the stronger the church is going to be. As a person committed to empowering others, Karee wants power to be in the hands of all the people.

Staffs with positive self-esteem had two equally acceptable ways of viewing power: influencing and persuading; and empowering others. The quality of the staff relationship was not affected by which style of power the staff members utilized.

Low Self-Esteem and Power

Staff members with low self-esteem tended to deny their power or to abuse it. Some staff members felt that their co-workers with low self-esteem were not honest about their true feelings and thoughts. Consequently the people with low self-esteem did not fully participate in the staff relationship, and the staff was unbalanced. Other staff members felt that co-workers with low self-esteem vented their feelings of frustration on them or acted coercively in order to make themselves feel more powerful or strong.

For example, Karee felt that Todd's main problem was low self-esteem. Karee believed that Todd was unreasonable and tried to push her around because he did not feel good about who he was. In Karee's perception, Todd could not treat her as an equal because he doubted his own skills and abilities. She believed that he was threatened by her and, thus, tried to compensate by continually telling her what to do.

Self-Esteem and Personal Power

Many of us struggle at times with low self-esteem, which can interfere with our personal and professional relationships. It is imperative that we learn to recognize the status of our self-esteem and the impact it has on our own working relationships. This section will enable you to: (1) assess your level of self-esteem; (2) reflect on how you can become more conscious of your power; (3) face your own feelings and experiences of powerlessness; and (4) assess how you can become more powerful in your personal and staff relationships.

Assessing Your Level of Self-Esteem

The truth was that neither Todd nor Karee had high self-esteem. They both vacillated between giving up their own power and abusing their power by coming on too strong with other people. They did not respect themselves as individuals or believe that God truly loved and accepted them as they were. They also did not believe that they were likeable to other people. Before Karee and Todd could become more aware of their power and deal openly with their respective abuses they each needed to cultivate more positive self-esteem and accept the grace of God's constant love for them as people of worth. Once healthy self-esteem is developed, each could then begin developing an awareness of their own power and how that affects their relationship.

In the same way, you need to begin to claim your personal power by assessing your own self-esteem. If you do not feel good about who you are, take the time to cultivate high self-esteem. Reread the chapter on self-esteem. Reflect on your strengths. Meditate, and open yourself to the assurance that in

God's eyes you are forgiven and loved just as you are. Believe and love yourself—not as a perfect person without sin, but as a forgiven person in the process of becoming all you are meant to be for the sake of the gospel. Once you accept that Jesus died and rose for you so that your life could be new, and trust that Christ sees you as a person of great value, you can have confidence in yourself as a person of worth in Christ Jesus, and you can begin developing confidence in yourself as a person of power.

Becoming Conscious of Your Personal Power

Personal power is the ability that God has given you in Christ Jesus to make intentional choices concerning your particular situations, actions, and emotions. Personal power means that through the Holy Spirit you have the power within yourself to consciously choose how to enhance your self-esteem. The key to understanding personal power is understanding that it is internal: *You* make choices within yourself and *you* are completely responsible for your feelings and experiences. Because of God's gracious love for you in Christ Jesus, you have the ability and power to make intentional choices for yourself and for your life.

You, like Karee, may not know your personal power. In order for you to better assess your power, reflect on your feelings and complete the following statements:

1. I enhance my self-esteem when I . . .
2. I feel powerful when . . .
3. When I feel powerful, others can tell because . . .

When Karee thought about these statements, she realized that she felt empowered by Christ and felt powerful when she stood up for her feelings and beliefs. She also recognized that when she felt a healthy sense of personal power, other people could tell because she was honest, faithful, and straightforward in her communication rather than just being nice and agreeable.

Facing Your Powerlessness

To further develop your own power, it is helpful to first reflect on what gets in your way of feeling powerful. Take a few minutes to reflect on your experiences of powerlessness. When do you feel powerless? With whom? How is your faith connected with feeling powerless? What do you feel inside yourself? What are you thinking? What do you say? What happens between you and the other people in the situation? Describe your posture, body language, and eye contact. How does the situation end? How do you express—verbally and nonverbally—feeling powerless? Sometimes tears are an expression of feeling powerless in a given situation. Crying may also serve to relieve tension. People who are able to cry may well be those people who have a sense of personal power because they are able to allow themselves to be in touch with painful feelings and to be vulnerable. Tears are an honest reaction to life.

The only times that Karee could recall feeling powerless were with male supervisors who were the age of her father. Karee thought about the times she felt powerless with Todd. She reflected on how she felt impotent in situations when she disagreed with him internally, but was not able to tell him how she really felt. She felt helpless, inept, disconnected from God's power and love for her, and afraid that she would never be able to respond with her real feelings. When she felt powerless with Todd, she would say nice things to him and "tune out" emotionally and spiritually while he continued talking. She would leave his office as soon as she could without facing her own feelings or letting him know what she was thinking. Her shoulders would be hunched forward and her posture would be poor. She felt vulnerable, inadequate, and far away from herself and from God.

Becoming More Powerful

"Enough is enough," Karee thought to herself one day. "It is time I start being honest with myself, with God, and with others. I need to start claiming my personal power." But the question for Karee and for all of us is, How do you claim your own personal power? I suggest a fourfold process:

1. Be honest with God and yourself and identify and articulate your feelings clearly, honestly, and directly.

2. Ask God to give you the strength and courage to examine your fears of powerfulness and powerlessness.
3. Assess whether your beliefs concerning power are valid for you today.
4. Identify the specific areas of your life in which you would like to develop more power.

Identify and Articulate Your Feelings Clearly. Knowing how you feel and being able to communicate your genuine feelings with God and with another human being are crucial to claiming personal power. In order to learn how to communicate more effectively and how to become more powerful in stressful situations, try the following steps:

1. Identify your feelings, particularly negative feelings.
2. Claim your feelings by making "I feel" statements.
3. Be clear, direct, and honest in your feeling statements.
4. Maintain direct eye contact.
5. Keep your voice resolute and determined.
6. Use appropriate body language and good posture.

You, like Karee, may find this initially hard to do. Karee understood what she needed to do intellectually, but had a hard time looking at people straight-on and speaking her negative feelings clearly and firmly. Yet she decided to push herself to say "I feel angry" and "I feel hurt" when she was experiencing such feelings. She also decided to work at having good posture, eye contact, and a strong voice when she was expressing negative feelings. Karee knew, though, that this was only the beginning and she really needed to figure out what scared her about being powerful.

Examine Your Fears of Powerfulness and Powerlessness. You, like Karee, may be afraid of being powerful. Take a few minutes to reflect on what would happen if you were more powerful. Imagine what it might be like to be powerful. What does that image of power feel like to you? What are your fears of being powerful? Are these fears of power still operative and valid for your life today?

107

Karee tried to imagine what it might be like to be powerful, and the picture of a self-confident woman who spoke thoughtfully and firmly came to her mind. Karee felt good about the image. In order for that image to become a reality, though, she knew she needed to first address her own fears of power. She recognized that she was afraid that others would not like her if she asserted herself when she felt angry or hurt. She was afraid of being rejected. Yet Karee could not determine whether these fears were still valid for her today without first examining how and why she learned them.

Identify Your Beliefs about Power. In looking further at your own beliefs about power, reflect on what you were raised to think about yourself and power. How did your family, friends, and teachers respond when you asserted yourself and stated your negative feelings? Would the people in your life today respond in a similar way? What do you believe today about yourself as a powerful person? How is your faith in Christ connected to your view of yourself as a person of power?

As Karee thought about her beliefs about power, she had an "Aha" experience. She suddenly realized that as a child she was punished each time she said anything negative. She remembered that whenever she stood up for herself, her parents would say, "Be nice." "You're not acting like a young lady." "If you don't have anything positive to say, don't say anything at all." As she was growing up, she felt that she had never been affirmed or accepted when she expressed her negative feelings. While she recognized that her adult friends and colleagues would probably not react in the same way, she was not sure that they would find her acceptable if she really talked about how she felt. Since it was unacceptable for her to have angry feelings in her family growing up, she was afraid of expressing such feelings in her adult life.

It was important for Karee to see this connection to her family of origin, for Karee knew that all people were not like her parents, and now her family rules could no longer be an excuse to hide her true feelings from people. She decided to risk being rejected in order to experience genuine relationships in which she could express her negative feelings and claim her personal power.

Identify Areas in Which You Would Like to Develop Power. To fully claim your personal power, you need first to identify the specific areas in your life in which you would like to develop more power. After assessing where you need to change, you now need to be intentional about seeking what you need.

Karee needed to be more assertive and honest about her negative feelings. Rather than storing them inside herself, she decided to start expressing her feelings with the people closest to her. Karee particularly wanted more power in her professional relationships and she desired to be more faithful and honest in her communication. She would begin her power development by stating her feelings clearly with her colleagues; establishing better posture, voice tone, and eye contact; identifying her fears but not allowing them to rule her life; and understanding the origin of her fears while recognizing that they are not valid for her today.

Sexuality and Power

Issues of power and self-esteem, complicated in any staff, can be more pressing in the dynamics of staffs which are composed of women and men. The ways in which women and men interact in staff situations will be explored in depth in the next chapter.

9
WORKING TOGETHER AS WOMEN AND MEN

Each one of us has been made a part of God's good creation. And, being bodies, each one of us is sexual. God has made us sexual beings and that is good. Very often, however, in our journey of faithfulness with God and others, our sexuality is cause for conflict in interpersonal relationships. This is due in large part to our inability as a modern western society to deal openly and honestly with—and to affirm—our sexuality as a healthy aspect of who we are as whole and holy people.

All human relationships are sexual to some extent, as we are all sexual beings. Whether same-sex or mixed-sex, all staffs deal with sexuality as a very real part of their working relationship. Because of the possibility of romantic and/or family-like overtones, the female/male sexuality dynamic can be a particularly troublesome one for church staffs. While what is said in the rest of this chapter may be applied to same-sex working relationships, it is this female/male dynamic on which we will focus.

Women and men interact with one another in staff settings in a variety of ways. My research shows four distinct roles that women assume in relating to men: emotional supporter, parent/child, sexual/romantic partner, or colleague. None of these are necessarily exclusive of the others. For instance, a woman whose role in the staff relationship is as the "daughter" may also find herself called upon to be the emotional supporter of her male colleague. A man who interacts with his female staff person in a collegial manner may also find that there is a certain degree of emotional support necessary to maintain the quality of that relationship.

Emotional Supporter

Marie came away from her weekly staff meeting feeling frustrated. She had hoped to discuss her plans for the Lenten season with her colleague, but it seemed that Ed wanted her to listen to him and provide nurturing, care, and emotional support. It had happened many times before. Often Marie didn't mind since the relationship was good otherwise, but lately it had been happening too often.

Marie had chosen "prayer" as the theme for their midweek Lenten services. She had chosen the texts to be used and had set up a tentative preaching schedule, hoping to finalize the plans this morning. Shortly, however, after Ed arrived in her office, their discussion of logistics turned into a conversation about prayer.

Ed said, "Oh, yes, I think prayer is a good theme for Lent. Since Lent is a rather contemplative time, the people in our parish will probably appreciate an opportunity to reflect on their own prayer lives. Actually, I don't know of anybody who'd say that they are satisfied with their prayer life. What do you think?"

Marie agreed that it probably was a difficult area for many people, as it was for her.

"You know," Ed continued, "part of the problem with our prayer lives is that we misunderstand what prayer is supposed to do for us."

"Yes," Marie responded. "That's really true. Well, let's start talking about how we are going to do this. . . ."

Ed interrupted her, "You know about the problems that our youngest daughter is having with alcohol and drug abuse. Everybody seems to know that she was arrested and in jail for the weekend. I guess that's natural in a small town like this. But I can't tell you how many people have asked, 'Pastor, have you prayed about her?' Frankly, I think we need to be doing more than praying. I don't know what we can do, but it's really hard on the family. She is so angry and belligerent. When we talk with her about anything, it's like pulling teeth to get her to respond. We want to help her, but she refuses to do anything that we suggest."

As Ed continued talking, Marie closed her notebook in which she had written her notes about the Lenten services. She realized that she was angry and needed to talk with Ed about how she felt. She was frustrated about not being able to discuss prayer with him. She also decided that this problem was a female/male issue and that she often took on the role of emotional supporter for him. She did not want it to become a pattern in their relationship and decided to bring it up in their discussion.

Women in female/male staff relationships frequently comment that they feel pressure to be the emotionally supportive partner on the staff. Part of the reason for this, it appears, has to do with the stereotype of women as nurturing and supportive. These qualities, women's unique gifts to ministry, can become liabilities within the dynamics of the staff relationship. This is especially true in a relationship with a male who needs to be "mothered," supported, and praised, and who otherwise might be "crushed" or overpowered by the woman with whom he works closely. It is also especially true in a relationship with a woman whose self-esteem is contingent on being "needed" and appreciated for her mothering, nurturing, and care-giving abilities.

In the situation with Marie and Ed, the assumption that the woman should be the emotional supporter took on the characteristics of a manipulative relationship. Ed transformed what was intended to be a strictly organizational meeting into a time when he could discuss his own agenda. Under the guise of affirmation for Marie's ideas about Lent, he proceeded to use her time to share his own family problems. For the sake of illustration, this scenario has been presented in a particularly blatant fashion. Yet situations such as these are rarely so blatant, which makes them all the more insidious. It feels good to be needed and trusted with the problems and issues facing a colleague. It would be unfair, therefore, to lay all of the responsibility for this situation on Ed. Marie is having needs of her own met as well by fostering this type of relationship with Ed.

Nonetheless, to allow this type of emotional dependency to continue within a clergy or staff relationship will only invite problems. This situation encourages an unequal distribution of power within the relationship, which inevitably leads to resentment and contempt for one's colleague. When the stereotype of nurturing female/weak male is quietly reinforced and modeled as appropriate, the relationship is emotionally stilted and destructive.

While some of us may have a tendency toward developing emotionally nurturing relationships that become unbalanced, God does offer us power in Christ to develop relationships that are more healthy, balanced, and collegial. A beginning point for us is to truly believe that we are loved by God for who we are and not what we do or how we care for others. Our worth is found in Christ, not in our performance or behavior. When one of us slips into the role of the "nurturing female" or the "needing-caretaking male," we need to look honestly at our own needs, discuss our perceptions with our colleague, remind ourselves of who we are in Christ Jesus, and pray that God will empower us to relate with more mutuality as forgiven, whole, and holy people of God.

Parent/Child

After a church council meeting in which Karee had made a major presentation on adult educational programming, Todd came up to Karee, cleared his throat, and said: "Nice presentation." Karee was shocked since he had rarely complimented her before. Feeling affirmed, she said, "Thank you."

Then Todd said, "You know, we did a family enrichment program about eight years ago that sounds similar to your plans." Todd continued talking nonstop for fifteen minutes about resource people and former parishioners active in the program. Karee was irritated but said nothing and instead she kept her thoughts to herself. "He's trying to be helpful and his initial comments were worthwhile, but he's now been talking on and on about people I've never heard of. He hasn't even stopped to see if I have any questions or if I'm still interested. I don't want to cut him off, but I have to leave." Karee could feel her emotions starting to boil inside. "I am so frustrated! How do I get out of here?"

About 30 minutes later, Karee said, "It was nice talking with you. Thanks for telling me about the past programs and the people involved. It's helpful getting the whole picture."

Todd responded, "Well, it's beneficial for you to know some of what's transpired in this parish prior to your coming. There's so much that I know about the people and their families, and about why some programs have worked and others have failed. I'm glad I can tell you about the history of these things so you can have a better idea of this parish."

Karee said, "Well, thanks again. I'm tired and am going to head home to bed." Todd said, "Good night. See you in the morning."

Karee was so mad as she drove home that she was muttering to herself. "Eeeee! How can he be so insensitive and talk on and on and on *at* me?? Working with him is driving me crazy!" When she got home, she felt her emotions still churning inside. She decided to call her younger sister, Kimberly.

Kimberly answered the phone and asked "What's up?" Karee's distress was immediately evident as she began talking. After ten minutes of agitated complaining about Todd, Karee started calming down and became more reflective, "I can't figure out what gets me so angry, but I think it's related to how he treats me like a daughter rather than a colleague."

Kimberly said, "And, actually, you get quite angry with Dad on a regular basis, too."

Karee responded, "Yes, that's true. I think Todd triggers stuff in me that I haven't resolved with Dad. There's nobody who can make me this angry besides Todd and Dad."

Kimberly asked, "What's the similarity, do you think?"

Karee thought for a few minutes, felt pain in her stomach, and said, "I want to be cared about, respected, and appreciated. I need to actually hear the words, maybe more than most people. And I think I've always wanted to hear it from Dad. I don't know if I ever met with his approval. Dad's approval and Todd's approval are really important to me."

Kimberly was silent and Karee kept thinking and then said, "I would guess that Todd's needs are similar to mine, and that he tries to get me to respect and appreciate him by 'telling' me things and 'advising' me about situations. I resent being told what to do because then I think he doesn't respect me or my ability. I want to be treated as a colleague, not as a daughter. The only way he knows how to relate to me and maybe to people in general, or maybe just women, is as a father—guiding, protecting, advising."

Todd and Karee are an example of another common way in which female and male staff members in ministry interact, that is, as parent and child. This seems to be an issue particularly in those situations where a male senior pastor and a female associate (lay or clergy) are the ages appropriate for a "father/daughter" relationship. For many women this type of relationship is more tolerable than a relationship based on emotional support, because there is a great deal of positive feedback that occurs in father/daughter relationships. Furthermore, senior pastors in this situation tend not to view the woman colleague as a threat, so overt power struggles are often avoided.

Yet, in this type of situation, a truly collegial relationship in ministry is impossible. The male partner assumes more responsibility for the ministry than might be appropriate. Not only does he shoulder his own responsibilities, but he also assumes some responsibility for his "daughter/colleague." Ultimately, there is an implicit message, "I have final authority, because I am the parent in this situation." Because of his need to praise and protect his woman staff member, his tasks become burdensome. Honest and equitable communication between them becomes increasingly difficult, if not impossible.

For women in this type of relationship, the pressure mounts for her to continue to please her "father/colleague." If she is like many women, her relationship with her father is carried over into the workplace. The desire to "please" and to "make him proud" can outweigh the human need for independent action. She assumes a role of less authority, and relinquishes her own responsibility to her colleague.

Romantic Interest

Sheila and Ed had been together in a staff ministry for four years. The first two years were difficult and stressful, but during the past two years their relationship had become much more satisfactory. Yet, they had also discovered that there might be additional problems in their relationship. It was not that Ed treated Sheila as a daughter, or was emotionally supported by her. The problem was that they were "too close." Too often, each depended upon the other a little too much. They had spent a great deal of time with one another—not only at the church, but during their time off as well.

What had developed into a close working relationship soon evolved into a close personal relationship. Sheila was scared because she recognized the possibility that they might become involved with each other in a romantic way. It became apparent to both that the emotional intimacy of their relationship also carried with it the constant temptation of sexual intimacy. The attraction was there. So were the problems. Since they had been getting along so well, Ed had been, as he termed it, "sentimental" in the way in which he interacted with Sheila. He marked achievements in their ministry by purchasing gifts or flowers for her. He was always trying to surprise her. Sheila played the game with Ed. At first, when their conversation was punctuated with innuendo, Sheila played a naive role, encouraging the conversation by ignoring the underlying messages. In hindsight, of course, she could see the problems caused by her initial unwillingness to raise important questions.

Ed also was uncomfortable with this relationship. He found it difficult to work so closely with Sheila without wanting to become close to her sexually. At first, he was flattered by her attention and her willingness to flirt with him. That had been a way for them to break the ice of their newly formed staff relationship. As time went on, however, the playfulness of their flirting came to take on new meaning for Ed. Things at home were becoming increasingly tense with his wife, so Ed found a certain degree of affirmation in Sheila's attention to him.

Sheila and Ed were not willing to risk their professional relationship because of their romantic attraction. Sheila decided to take the risk of discussing her feelings honestly with Ed. She was afraid to talk with him about her feelings, but she was even more afraid of what might eventually happen between them if the issue were not addressed.

It would be naive to think that staff relationships, even in the ministry, are free from sexual overtones. Because we are created as sexual beings, we carry that sexuality with us into every area of our lives. The fact that we assume positions in the church as clergy or lay professionals does not preclude the very real possibility that we will experience sexual feelings and attractions for other people. In fact, the intimacy experienced in a covenant community of faithful, Christ-centered staff very naturally can lead to physical, sexual attraction. Sexual energy can be a very creative and exciting dimension of a relationship. As holy and whole people in Christ Jesus, we embrace all dimensions of our being, including our sexuality. Problems occur, however, when those dynamics are not identified and faced in an open, honest way by the individuals experiencing them.

117

While the romantic/sexual dimension of staff ministry was seen as a problem to a small minority of the people I interviewed, it is a dynamic that women and men working together need to be aware of. Inappropriate sexual dynamics between parish staff members can create havoc within the staff relationship and within the congregation.

My research found that opinions are mixed on whether to discuss one's sexual attraction with the other person. The majority of women interviewed believed it is imperative to discuss such volatile and significant issues, while most men believed the subject was better left alone. There may be less tension if the issue is addressed; however, addressing the issue can add an awkwardness to the relationship.

While it is not imperative or necessarily appropriate for people to have an open, honest discussion concerning their attraction, it is vital that all people experiencing sexual attraction identify and face their own feelings, fears, and tensions. Sexual attraction for colleagues is not the problem. The problem arises when we don't recognize our feelings and/or when we act irresponsibly and inappropriately.

Both Sheila and Ed were aware of the sexual dynamics growing between them. Neither felt comfortable discussing the situation, but both knew they needed to talk about it together. Sheila felt strongly attracted to him. When she decided to discuss it with him, she got knots in her stomach just thinking about it.

Ed knew how he felt about Sheila, but had tried not to think too much about the whole situation. He wanted to be open with her, but at the same time he thought if he didn't mention the situation to Sheila, their relationship could continue as good friends and their attraction would not really have to be an issue. He liked Sheila very much and felt stimulated by their professional and personal relationship. He was afraid that talking about their attraction would change the nature of their relationship and make the whole situation awkward. He didn't want to risk their friendship. In addition, he didn't want to talk with Sheila about something he couldn't talk about with his wife. Yet he knew such strong feelings needed to be addressed since he was committed to open communication.

Neither Ed nor Sheila talked with anyone else about their feelings. They both felt like volcanos about ready to erupt. The situation was emotionally unhealthy for both because they were keeping all their feelings in. It was for this reason that Sheila decided to discuss the subject with Ed.

Sheila told Ed that she needed to talk with him and asked if he had time that same day. He was concerned about what she wanted and since he was free at that moment, he told Jean not to disturb them. Sheila began by saying, "I am struggling with a problem of being sexually attracted to you." There was silence and then they began discussing the issue.

The conversation was awkward, intense, and painful for both of them. Yet they faced the issues honestly together and decided that they would covenant with each other concerning how to live out their relationship as colleagues. They made conscious decisions concerning what was appropriate for them as faithful people of God.

We, like Sheila and Ed, may at some time face the difficulty of working closely with someone to whom we are sexually attracted. It is not easy. But as a community centered in Christ, we have covenanted to be open and honest with ourselves and with others. Regardless of whether we discuss our feelings with others, we must be honest with ourselves about our own sexual attraction for others. We are empowered by the Holy Spirit to face and accept ourselves, and to make faithful decisions of integrity as people of God who have covenanted to live and work together in trust and openness.

Colleagues

Karee had struggled for a long time with her tendencies toward perfectionism. In college and seminary, these tendencies had driven her to excel as a student. They also benefited her a great deal in her work in parish ministry and hospital chaplaincy. She recognized the value of these tendencies within herself. But she was also acutely aware of how difficult they made her life at times.

That was why she appreciated Walt as a colleague. Walt seemed to have healthy and strong self-esteem and was able to share power and responsibility. While he did not want a close personal relationship with any of the staff members, and Karee wanted to be closer with Walt and the others, Karee felt that she and Walt could communicate well on a professional level. She felt that they interacted with trust, respect, and concern.

Walt had a great deal of insight into the importance of rest and relaxation, and took his day off seriously. Walt was good for Karee in this respect. He was able to model what Karee wished for herself—the ability to play and a realistic attitude toward perfectionism. He did not, however, pressure Karee to change. Rather, he encouraged her to make changes at her own pace.

Walt had a great deal of respect for Karee as a colleague. She had outstanding organizational ability—something he lacked but valued highly in others. She was thoroughly professional in her ministry, and supportive of him in his.

Walt respected Karee's skills and interests. Even though technically Todd was in charge of all programs, one of Karee's roles was to supervise Walt's educational ministry programs. She related to him as a partner and colleague, one who could be trusted to develop creative and challenging programs in Christian education for children and adults. The whole staff met weekly to become familiar with each other's programs. Walt felt good about the staff relationship. Todd was clearly the senior pastor, but Karee, Walt, and Laura were full members of the staff.

Although Karee and Walt were not close friends outside the context of the congregation, their rapport within the church was excellent. They had a common appreciation for humor, and the closeness in their ages made it easier for them to communicate as peers. Their relationship was collegial and they did not seem to experience struggles relating paternally/ maternally, romantically, or in emotionally dependent ways.

The individuals interviewed as part of my research reported that there are a number of factors which serve to enhance a collegial relationship: high self-esteem; ability to share leadership; ability to communicate effectively; ability to listen to one another; and a clear delineation of areas of responsibility and accountability within the congregation. Also important are dimensions such as respect, trust, and mutual support. The fact that these colleagues are close in their professional relationships but are not dependent upon them for friendship and support also seems to be a key to a truly collegial relationship.

Collegial relationships are ideal for people working together in ministry. Collegial relationships of mutuality involve people trusting what God says about them as special, forgiven, and holy people, and relating with others with a good sense of one's self apart from the pastoral or staff relationship. If the staff relationship is the primary source of identity or the primary relationship for any of the staff members, the tendencies toward emotionally dependent, parental, or romantic interaction become heightened. If, however, all of the staff members have a good sense of themselves as individuals, there is a strong basis for a truly collegial relationship of mutuality, wholeness, and holiness to develop among them.

Communication

We have seen in the preceding chapters how the messages we send and receive have a profound impact in shaping our self-esteem and the effectiveness of our staff relationships. Communication patterns established in family systems impact the functioning of staff systems in a significant way. As a vital issue in staff relationships, verbal and nonverbal communication has an influence on covenant making, covenant keeping, identifying role and staff expectations, and the ability of staff members to live and work as a gospel community of faithful, forgiven people. Chapters 10 and 11 will examine how communication is a significant dynamic in staff relationships. Chapter 10 examines the negative styles of communication that we all have a tendency to adopt when we are hurt, angry, afraid, or stressed, and which interfere with the development of good staff relationships. Chapter 11 explores the specific ways in which we can develop more healthy, honest, and congruent communication so that we can better cultivate and maintain good quality staff relationships.

10

DISCOVERING YOUR NEGATIVE COMMUNICATION STYLES___

Communication is a means of building bridges among people. Whether verbal or nonverbal, the messages we send and receive help us to better understand one another, and more effectively work together as a covenant community in Christ Jesus. They help, that is, if our style of communication is positive and constructive rather than negative or destructive. Let's make another visit to First Lutheran.

Karee and Todd were at it again. This time the topic under discussion was the adult Bible study program. Todd was telling Karee that she could only teach courses based directly on specific books in the Bible.

Even though Karee was boiling with anger at Todd and was sure that she did *not* want to do what he was suggesting, she said to him, "Whatever you want to do is fine with me. Your suggestion sounds good."

Karee provides a perfect example of how *not* to communicate. Unfortunately, Karee's reaction is typical, and many parish staffs communicate with each other in equally nongenuine, indirect ways.

Placating, blaming, being overly reasonable, and being irrelevant are labels developed by Virginia Satir, a family systems and communication therapist, to describe destructive styles of communication.[1]

These ways of communication are developed during childhood in order to cope with family situations and interfere with our relating as faithful, forgiving, and holy people of God. You probably learned one of these communication styles in order to relate with family, friends, and teachers, particularly when you experienced stress and tension. As coping mechanisms that helped you get through difficult times, these ways of communication illustrate how you feel about yourself, and how you handle your personal power.[2]

The problem is that your self-esteem, personal power, and ability to relate as a whole and holy person are not ultimately strengthened through placating, blaming, being overly reasonable, or being irrelevant. In such communication, you don't live as though you accept and trust the good news of God's grace and forgiveness for you and for your colleagues, and you don't feel good about yourself or about them. A great deal of frustration and anger often develops and the staff relationship is subsequently sabotaged.

The constructive alternative is to focus on God's grace and unconditional love and forgiveness for you and for all people. With that foundation you can better learn how to communicate openly and honestly so that your words match your feelings, so that your words and feelings are what Satir calls congruent. Congruent communication is a straightforward, direct, and honest expression of who you are. When you communicate more openly, you feel better about yourself and your staff. Congruent communication is a far better method of developing understanding and building staff relationships than the negative and destructive communication styles so often used. Let's look more closely at some negative styles so we can better recognize how and what to change.

Placating

Karee fits the placating role well: she does not truly believe that she is a worthwhile and lovable person. Deep within herself, she feels worthless and inadequate. While on the exterior she seems to be competent and bright, she believes that she needs to prove herself in order to be liked and respected. Karee is constantly trying to measure up to what she perceives to be the expectations of others. She wants to please others at all costs, and often it is at the cost of giving up herself, her opinions, and her feelings. Since Karee does not believe that she truly is worthwhile, she does not let people know her genuine feelings or thoughts because she thinks that they would probably reject her. Even when she is very upset, she is overly agreeable and "nice" in order to be accepted and liked by others.

It can be highly frustrating to work with placaters because they never show how they are really feeling or what they are thinking. An authentic, genuine relationship with a placater is quite difficult because placaters will not let you know who they really are.

If you are a placater or are working with a placater, the key to a better staff relationship is to understand the benefits of being a placater. As a placater, you or your colleague may be gaining:

- protection from being truly known and consequently rejected by others;
- a sense of worth from pleasing others;
- acceptance as a person by "acting" in ways that make you look very impressive on the exterior;
- relationships which appear to be without any significant conflicts; and
- confirmation that you are a fine servant of God—dedicated, pleasing, nice.

It is also important, however, to examine your losses if you take on the placater role. Personal losses may include:

- giving up who you are, your feelings, your thoughts;
- becoming a "nobody" in order to get along with others;

- becoming worthless since you have given up yourself;
- no longer having any personal power;
- not believing God's promise that you are worthwhile, forgiven, and holy;
- always having to act a role;
- always having to be pleasing and agreeable.

Blaming

"You don't listen to me," Todd said to Karee. "You ignore my suggestions and go out and do whatever you want. I've told you what the best approach is with these people, and I know because I've been the senior pastor here for 22 years. You aren't doing what I think you should be doing when you call on these folks."

Todd fits the blamer role. Everything that went wrong is usually blamed on someone else. Todd, who has a need to feel strong and important, deals with his low self-esteem by taking on as much power as possible and acting superior to everybody else.

Many people in ministry slip into the role of blamer when they are stressed. As you look at yourself and how you interact with your staff members when you are stressed, reflect on whether you put the blame on others and what you gain from such action. As a blamer you may be receiving:

- a feeling of superiority;
- a sense of being the "boss";
- a belief that you know what is best for others;
- total control;
- affirmation that others are always wrong.

Todd gives up a great deal by always having to be in charge and right about everything. If you, like Todd, need to be a blamer and always right, you give up:

- letting people know your feelings, hurts, and fears;
- facing your own fears and resolving them;
- genuine, caring, two-way relationships with people;
- respect for who you are rather than fear of your power;

- knowing the freedom of relating as people of equal worth in Christ Jesus; and
- relaxed, enjoyable relationships with colleagues.

Todd, like Karee, is insecure. Actually, Todd and Karee are very much alike. The Myers-Briggs Type Indicator (MBTI) reveals that they both are E (extroverted), N (intuitive), F (feeling), and J (judging) personality types, and are thereby quite similar in their attitudes and values. The main difference between them is that Todd deals with his low self-esteem by blaming and controlling others, while Karee turns inward, placates, and gives up her feelings in order to be agreeable with everyone.

If Todd and Karee could remind themselves, as individuals and as staff members, that they are of equal worth in Christ and that they are forgiven, holy people of God, it may be that they could trust each other more as colleagues and talk more honestly together about their own hopes, dreams, fears, and inner feelings. Through refocusing on who they are in Christ and speaking openly with one another, it is likely that they could become colleagues who trust and respect each other. Instead, they both protect themselves with barricades (the roles of placating and blaming) so that their real selves are hidden. When Todd disagrees or blames Karee for something, Karee internalizes it, and acts sweetly to Todd while inwardly seething. Todd continues offering his "superior" knowledge, not sensing how it riles Karee. Karee, in turn, keeps all her feelings within herself, and the cycle continues over and over again.

Being Overly Reasonable

"Talking with Ed is sometimes like talking with a computer," Marie exclaims. "He is so analytical and logical at times, and so much into structuring ministry and relationships, that he is like a computer. Today he talked to me about all the intellectual and logical reasons why parents need to improve their child-rearing techniques."

Ed, who is the senior pastor, told Marie, the associate pastor, "Parents must set more limits with their kids. When I was raising our kids, I was never loose and unconcerned about rules and curfews like parents are today. Parents of today need to raise their kids as I did, having a set of rules and responsibilities and sticking with them."

When stressed, you or one of your colleagues may have a tendency to become overly rational and analytical. You may find yourself ignoring your feelings, the feelings of others, as well as the feelings of how God and your faith relate to the situation. You may concentrate on the issue at hand and deal with it in a very intellectual and logical fashion, rather than considering your values, your faith, or people. If you are an "overly reasonable" communicator like Ed, you benefit from your style or you wouldn't use it. Your benefits may include:

- a feeling of being more knowledgeable than others;
- a feeling of being strong and rational;
- being structured and nonemotional in your thinking;
- not letting feelings get in the way;
- finding safety in obedience to moral standards;
- feeling superior to other people; and
- feeling intellectual.

While Ed didn't realize it, he was giving up a lot in order to be overly reasonable, rational, and above everybody else. You also might find that as an overly reasonable communicator, you may be giving up things similar to what Ed gave up:

- being in touch with your own feelings;
- being aware of the feelings of others;
- having passion in your life;
- having equal, balanced friendships;
- having collegial relationships with shared roles;
- having visions of what could be;
- creativity in your own life;
- being faithful to your values and to God; and
- warmth in relationships.

Being Irrelevant

During the first few years of Sheila's ministry, she was clearly an irrelevant communicator. While she has developed better communication patterns, she still struggles with slipping back into a poor communication style. The following scene took place during Sheila's first year of ministry with Ed and Jean.

Vivacious, warm, and friendly, Sheila was bouncing from subject to subject with Jean, the church secretary. Jean had stopped listening because it was too confusing. She felt that Sheila was talking about everything except what she needed to give her attention to. Jean thought to herself, "Sheila is acting so scatterbrained today. She's flitting from one trivial topic to another. I know she's bright and competent, yet she's acting like a child. I wonder what her off-the-wall behavior is all about?"

The irrelevant communicator reverts to this mode of communication in times of stress. Being irrelevant is a way of emotionally "checking-out" of situations and relationships. Jean noted it well, "Sheila is talking on and on, but her words don't make much sense."

If you are an irrelevant communicator, you may benefit by:
• always being fun and enjoyable;
• never being responsible;
• disregarding others' thoughts and feelings;
• keeping others confused about who you are;
• enjoying spontaneous, unstructured activities;
• ignoring your spirituality and relationship with God; and
• ignoring your own feelings and thoughts.

Sheila, like other irrelevant communicators, is scared. She keeps everything in turmoil so she doesn't ever have to risk finding out who she really is.

If, like Sheila, you maintain all this chaos in your communication, you lose many things:

- developing a sense of yourself;
- discovering who you really are;
- finding out that others care about you;
- having meaningful relationships with people;
- being a true colleague;
- knowing love and trust;
- knowing what others think and feel; and
- feeling more connected with God.

Summary of Destructive Communication Styles

In the final analysis, all four communication styles—placating, blaming, being overly reasonable, and being irrelevant—are similar and interfere with staff members relating as whole and holy people in Christ. People who communicate this way do so to counteract feelings of low self-esteem and low self-confidence. They do not truly believe they are worthwhile people whom others would enjoy working with and knowing. Problems with communication arise from low self-esteem and not fully accepting the grace, forgiveness and new life offered in Christ Jesus. This further influences staff issues such as power and authority. Whatever their source, such negative styles of communication are counterproductive to effective staff relationships. These negative styles need to be identified and dealt with by the staff as individuals and as a group.

11

BECOMING A CONGRUENT COMMUNICATOR

Although it took them over a year, Ed, Marie, Sheila, and Jean have learned how to communicate in a faithful, congruent, and healthy way with each other. Consider the Advent planning incident. Ed, as senior pastor, asked the staff for their ideas on long-range planning. Marie, the associate, suggested that they begin to plan the Advent services and described her ideas for a new kind of worship service. Ed wasn't sure the congregation was ready for something so nontraditional. Sheila, the youth and education director, challenged Ed. She said that perhaps the real issue was that *he* wasn't ready for something so nontraditional. Ed admitted to the staff that maybe Sheila was right and he might not be ready. Marie pointed out the ways in which the new Advent services might work, while Jean, the secretary, supported the idea in spite of the additional work it would entail. All four of the staff members communicated openly their thoughts, feelings, ideas, and visions. Through such direct and congruent communication, they reached a consensus about the Advent services and were ready to explore the next steps.

What Is Congruent Communication?

Congruent communication is a way of describing healthy, open communication, that was originally developed by Virginia Satir.[1] It involves honest conversation which may at times be confrontational, challenging, or supportive. In such communication, the words people use correspond with their feelings so that angry or depressed people do not look or sound joyful. Congruent communication enhances self-esteem and self-confidence, strengthens personal power, enhances personal and staff wholeness and holiness, and facilitates the development of trust, respect, and collegiality in staff relationships. These are all important elements of a healthy staff relationship.

Developing Congruent Communication

Communicating congruently enables staffs to function well together. Faithful, congruent communication is evident in relationships where the members tell each other when they disagree and intentionally work at communicating in a straightforward manner. Unhealthy and dysfunctional staff systems develop when there are mixed verbal and nonverbal messages and when staff members use the negative communication styles of placating, blaming, being irrelevant, or being overly rational. Noncongruent communication with mixed messages and negative communication styles creates turmoil and dysfunction within staff systems. This is evident when staff members talk about their tendency to adopt a negative communication style such as placating because they are afraid to be honest with the other staff members. Dysfunctional staff relationships are also seen when staff members give their co-workers conflicting messages.

Karee and Todd had a dysfunctional staff relationship, while Todd, Walt, and Laura generally had a functional, faithful, congruent relationship. As with Karee and Todd, most staff members want to have open communication with their co-workers but are also at times afraid of such honest communication, or are used to the habit of a negative communication style. Due to fear or habit, staff members sometimes inadvertently slip into giving mixed messages and placating, blaming, being irrelevant, or being overly rational.

God's grace and forgiveness empowers us to communicate more congruently, and clear communication is a vital element in the quality of multiple staff relationships. While members of female/male parish staffs are particularly concerned about communication dynamics, the majority of all staff members interviewed believed that effective communication is primary in the success of their staff relationships. This perspective is stated well by Associate Pastor Marie Reilly, "Taking the time to sit down and communicate feelings and thoughts cannot be emphasized enough. The success of our staff relationship is very much related to communicating on a regular, intentional, and honest basis."

In my research, I found a direct correlation between how staff members perceive staff communication and their satisfaction with their staff relationships. For example, those who perceived that their staff communicated well also felt that staff relationships were good. Conversely, those who were unhappy with the communication of their staff were also unhappy with their staff relationships. The following example illustrates the major role communication plays in the quality of parish staff relationships.

A Placater and Blamer Seek Congruent Communication

Senior Pastor Todd Swanson, a blamer, and Associate Pastor Karee Lange, a placater, never really listened to each other until the day Karee told Todd that she was going to interview for another position. Todd felt terribly upset that she was thinking about leaving, because he felt she was running out on him when he still had so much to teach her.

He asked her why she was leaving. She responded more honestly than she ever had before. She said, "I feel like my hands are tied here and there's nothing that I can do on my own. I feel like you have never trusted me."

Todd frowned and said, "You haven't really been honest with me. It was really hard to know what was going on with you. You've been angry with me, but you've never told me you were. You haven't shown me that I could trust you and you haven't always done what I've asked you to do."

Karee spoke slowly, "You're right. It's often been hard for me to be honest with you about what I'm feeling. I have been open with you at times, though. I guess one thing that has bothered me is that you never seemed to want or be able to listen to me."

Todd sighed and said, "What do you mean? I'm always here and available to talk."

Karee said, "Listening. I haven't felt that you've been able to listen to me."

Todd responded, "I'm sorry. I'm not sure I understand, but I'd be willing to work on it. I don't want you to leave."

Karee began crying, and said incredulously to Todd, "You'd want me to stay? I had no idea you really valued any of my ministry here."

Todd put his head in his hands. "Good grief," he said in a tired voice. "You didn't know I would want you to stay?" he asked with disbelief.

Karee stated, "I know I haven't been perfect, but I've always felt that you make everything my fault. I didn't feel you respected or liked me, and I felt like you were always trying to tell me what to do. Somehow you became like my father and I resented that."

Todd felt a bit sick inside. He had no idea how Karee had been feeling and he thought of all the energy they had both wasted in being upset and frustrated with each other. Todd still felt that the problems between them were mostly her problems, but he realized that she had triggered some issues for him as well. He said to Karee, "I'm sorry. I do respect you— you have good skills—I just don't compliment people very easily. But I never knew what you were thinking, and you seemed so protective and secretive."

Karee was still crying. She realized that maybe they could have worked out their relationship if they had begun talking more honestly a bit earlier in their relationship. She felt sad that they had both experienced a lot of anger, hurt, and frustration in their relationship.

She responded to Todd, "You know, I have been afraid to tell you what I feel because I've been afraid that you would reject me. But what I'm realizing now is that maybe we could have worked better together if we had spent the time talking together and working at our communication."

Todd nodded his head and said, "I guess there can't be enough communication. I knew there were problems, but I didn't realize how bad things had gotten."

Karee thought quietly for a moment and then said, "I think I started to avoid you whenever possible, and neither one of us wanted to talk more than the bare minimum with each other. Maybe our downfall was that we never started by being honest with each other. It made matters worse when we stopped meeting on a regular basis."

Todd asked, "Any chance that you will stay?"

Karee took a few minutes to think and then said, "If we could work out better communication and a better way of dividing up our responsibilities, I'd consider staying. I really don't want to leave!"

Seeking Congruent Communication

When you speak congruently, your words match your feelings, tone of voice, body posture, and facial features. If you say you are pleased and it is not really true, you will convey your displeasure in a nonverbal, indirect manner. Faithful, congruent communication enhances self-esteem and facilitates healthy staff relationships. When members accept God's grace and feel good about themselves, their communication is usually congruent. Communication within a system reflects the self-esteem of the people in the system.[2]

When communication becomes incongruent, and mixed verbal and nonverbal messages are perceived, the system will become more and more dysfunctional. While mixed messages are likely to happen as part of human communication and may not lead to relationship problems, a continuing flow of mixed messages can lead to increasing turmoil and dysfunction. In addition, the people giving mixed messages often demonstrate their own lack of self-esteem and add to a lower level of self-esteem among other staff.

We have mentioned "mixed message" several times, but just what is it? A mixed message is transmitted when words do not match body language or feelings. It is often accompanied by a negative communication style such as placating, blaming, being irrelevant or overly rational. For example, when Karee was angry with Todd, her anger was evident through her tightly controlled body language and angry voice tone even though she was smiling while she was discussing her "slight feelings of irritation." Karee was placating and being agreeable when she really was quite angry. Another example of a mixed message was when Todd shouted at Karee, "I am not angry with you!" These mixed messages are clearly examples of noncongruent, indirect communication.

Developing General Communication Skills

Todd and Karee talked at length about how to develop more congruent communication skills in order to enhance their relationship. They decided to work on general communication skills. This included being more aware of the context, developing more directness in their communication, practicing good listening skills, sharing information, being intentional in their communication, and meeting weekly.

Context

Communication takes place in a complicated context that involves the location, the number of people involved, their intentions, the time of day or night, temperature, lighting, and the amount of physical space. The emotional atmosphere also affects the communication. Is it tense, cold, and threatening, or comfortable, warm, and friendly? All of these factors add up to the context, and consequently affect communication behavior.

While she had never said anything to Todd, Karee resented that all of her communication with Todd was at a time chosen by him in his office with a huge desk between them. She suggested meeting in a more neutral place in the church or taking turns meeting in each other's offices. She also said that she would prefer that they sat across from each other or next to each other in comfortable chairs without desks between them. Furthermore, she told him that meeting at 2:30 P.M. on Monday afternoons was not a good time for her, and she preferred morning meetings when she was more alert. Todd was open to these suggestions and startled that she had not mentioned any of these things before.

Karee had given away her personal power by letting Todd be completely in charge of their meetings. While she may have decided these were little things that she didn't want to hassle about with Todd, Karee's placating contributed to off-balanced communication so that she grew bitter about allowing Todd to have all the power. Ultimately she felt so powerless that she saw no other option but to consider leaving.

Directness

Direct and straightforward communication is an important dimension of faithful, holy relationships, and is vital to the successful functioning of any staff relationship. Directness requires honest verbal communication of your thoughts on topics about which you have strong feelings.

Do you articulate your ideas so that others know what you are expressing? Do the others on your staff know how you feel about important parish matters? Do you respond to others defensively or out of anger? Do you make eye contact with the other staff members when you speak? Do you keep the conversation to the topic being discussed? Or do you have a hard time being focused about what you are saying and end up rambling on in a confusing manner?

Senior pastors reported that the success of their multiple staff relationships was related to the degree to which staff members shared "bluntly" or "willingly." Nearly half of the senior pastors interviewed saw an "open door policy" of direct, honest communication as a vital priority in their staff relationships.

Almost all of the associate and co-pastors interviewed discussed how highly they prized direct communication with their colleagues. "Open and honest," "up front," and "straightforward" were characteristics mentioned by associates regarding communication styles they valued. Such communication was seen as a strength in their staff and enhanced the quality of their relationships.

Listening

To listen is to accurately interpret, both verbally and nonverbally, what the other staff members are saying. To listen is to give the other person your complete and undivided attention, to free your mind from other distractions, to completely focus on the other person's words and expressions, and to more fully love and respect the other person.

Todd usually answered the phone while he and Karee met. If he was on hold, he would try to continue talking and listening to Karee. While Walt, the lay professional on their staff, did not seem to mind Todd answering the phone while they met, Karee was offended. She perceived that Todd thought he was the important one in the relationship. She felt there was no way he could be attentively listening to her if he was also on the phone.

Do you take time to be fully present with the other staff members? Do you catch yourself wanting to hurry the conversation or to interrupt? Do you listen with your whole body—

facing the person, having eye contact, trying to tune out the other things going on in your life, and intentionally hearing and feeling what the other person is expressing? Lily Tomlin said it well, "Listen with the intensity that most people save for talking."

Sharing Information

Todd and Karee usually only had a vague idea about each other's ministry, and often had no idea about what they were each doing with the rest of their time. They did not communicate to each other about which parishioners were having difficulties, whom they had visited, what occurred at their meetings, and what was working well in the educational programming and various church groups. While Todd talked *to* Karee a great deal, he did not talk *with* her. Karee chose not to talk much with Todd because she perceived that he was always interrupting and giving her advice. Neither one really listened to the other, and neither made intentional efforts to share with the other what was going on in the ministry of their parish.

Intentional Communication

"Conscious" and "intentional" were words both senior pastors and associates in good staff relationships used to describe their communication with each other. They perceived that the strength of their staff relationship was contingent on their deliberate and planned efforts at communicating openly with each other.

Senior Pastor Ed Mantig said, "We keep nothing secret, we go back and forth, we make a very conscious effort to talk very openly together. We don't always agree, but we try to discuss our differences of opinion." He further stated, "I think we've consciously tried to do some things for staff building. We've worked with a psychologist to form a good foundation and we've continued the process of building our staff. So we're very conscious of what's happening in the dynamics among all of us. We talk often about the staff and how it's functioning.

We try to step back from it and analyze it. We'll go to lunch and talk about how we feel it's going."

The staff members who valued open communication said that their relationship could only be faithful to Christ and successful if open and honest communication was intentional. Youth and Education Director Sheila Simons stated, "It's like any relationship. It takes work. You have to be intentional about it to make it succeed and you try to work through whatever differences there are."

Members of church staffs recognized the importance of making conscious decisions to be honest and intentional. For example, Sheila said, "You've got to face up to a situation and be able to say how you feel about it and where you stand. I guess to some extent this means that from the first you have to be intentional about taking some risks. Maybe it's wise to start with the small risks, but you need to be willing to be open and to take the initiative and not let things go if it's an issue for you."

Being honest and intentional is not always easy. The good news, though, is that God continually empowers us to be more honest, faithful, and congruent with one another. As clergy and lay staff struggle with learning to be more whole and holy in their communication, they find that the ease of such communication is related to the importance of a particular issue for them and to the history of that concern in the parish and in the staff relationship.

Associate Pastor Marie Reilly described this difficulty in the following way: "We have an understanding that if you're not preaching and a funeral comes up, you do the funeral. A funeral came up and I was preaching and Ed asked if I'd do the funeral. I said, 'No, I can't, I'm preaching and I just can't get prepared for both at once.' We had a little discussion about that, but when it came down to it, he ended up doing it. I stood my ground and said, 'Wait a minute, what's really going on, and why don't you want to do this funeral?' Being able to work that through and not feel as though one person is being dumped on all the time or that one person is doing all the work or one person is slacking off is important. Intentional communication and being able to be honest about what's going on, personally, for each of us, is a real strength in our staff relationship."

Meeting Weekly

In my research, weekly meetings were viewed as very important because they provided the opportunity for informal conversations about professional issues for the exchange of information concerning weekly ministry events. Associate Pastor Marie Reilly summed it up well, "That weekly staff meeting is important. Really important, even if we don't have a lot to talk about. We use that time to get in touch with each other." Senior Pastor Ed Mantig said, "We may not have a lot to report or share sometimes, but it's just getting together and touching base, and talking about things we feel the others should know about people or programs."

Those who did not have weekly staff meetings talked about the problems they experienced as a result of not having regularly scheduled meetings. Associate Pastor Karee Lange said, "I think our weakest area is communication. I feel it is more important than Todd considers it to be. I would like more team work between the entire staff, and more ownership of the entire program by all of us. At times we're like the Lone Ranger, each of us going our own way, running with our own agendas. Most of the time it works out okay. But sometimes, like last Easter, it's a disaster. We failed to schedule enough planning time and no one felt ownership of the whole program."

Karee then added, "My working relationship with Todd might have progressed better if we had both been committed to meeting weekly as the pastoral staff, apart from the whole staff. I hated going to those meetings and listening to him talk, but I never said that. I just scheduled other appointments and meetings for when Todd and I usually had our meeting. Then we didn't have to deal with each other. We lost touch with each other. Our ministry is still fine, but it has been affected by both Todd's and my frustration, hurt, and anger with each other. Weekly meetings might have forced us to talk honestly with each other about how we were feeling long before the feelings became unmanageable and out of control." Such regularly scheduled meetings provide staffs an opportunity to identify potential problem areas before they become unmanageable and damaging to others.

God's Spirit helps us as we work on congruent communication. It takes real effort by all staff members, yet the benefits cannot be underestimated. Congruent communication is essential for staff members as they covenant with one another to relate as faithful, forgiven people in Christ and as they identify and discuss their own role and staff expectations. When staff and family systems are different, congruent communication can help staff members better understand each other's rules, roles, closeness/distance preferences, and conflict styles. In addition, congruent communication can enhance staff members' self-esteem, personal power, and leadership ability. Through open, honest communication, staff members can better manage conflict and relate as forgiven, faithful people in Christ.

12

MANAGING CONFLICT IN A FORGIVEN COMMUNITY

Throughout this book, conflict has given rise to, or was a result of, the various ineffective operating dynamics at First Lutheran Church or First United Methodist Church. Although conflict is a natural part of relationships, we have seen that there is a difference between constructive and destructive types of conflict. The covenant community is called on to behave as forgiven people and to creatively use all of God's resource gifts to us, even conflict. "All life is conflict," but there is a difference between "rigged" and "creative" conflict.[1]

Walt was disgusted and angry with the church secretary, Laura. "How could she have done such an incompetent thing?" he wondered to himself. Normally an easygoing, amiable lay member of the staff, Walt was obviously highly irritated with Laura. While Walt rarely got upset and even more rarely talked about his anger, he wanted to know what on earth was going on and promptly went into Laura's office to ask her.

Walt spoke directly with Laura, "Why didn't you mail the letters to the youth as I'd asked two weeks ago?" Laura was startled and asked, "What letters?" Walt exclaimed, "What letters??? All those letters I gave you concerning the upcoming District Youth Retreat. I had set the reservation date for today."

Laura said, "Oh, I didn't know there was a hurry. Pastor Swanson gave me the newsletter to put together about the same time and Pastor Karee asked me to send out those letters to all the people in Search Weekly Bible Study, and I guess I thought that work was what I was supposed to do first."

Walt became even angrier. He felt disrespected. He thought to himself, "So my work comes after the pastors' work!" He felt like yelling at Laura, but instead said, "So, can you change the reservation date to next Friday and get the letters out today?"

Conflict Is Natural

None of us are strangers to conflict. It is a natural part of our personal, professional, and congregational lives. Many of us, though, are afraid of conflict. We tend to view it as negative, and usually try to avoid it.

Walt believed that he should be nice to people and so normally did not bring up negative feelings. Yet he had strong negative feelings and needed to decide how he was going to deal with his anger. Walt's conflict with Laura needed to be managed.

Sometimes we think that to be Christian is to be "nice" and to avoid conflict. Yet, we need to remind ourselves who God calls us to be and what difference the risen Christ makes in our relationships.

We, like Walt, need to be reminded that God creates us to be people who make intentional choices—choices about how to best fulfill our needs. We need to assess our goals and then figure out how to seek our goals in our personal and professional lives.[2] For Walt and for all of us in church staff relationships, working in a staff community of faithful people means working in a community centered on Christ where the goals of the staff and congregation can be openly and honestly pursued. Managing conflict creatively is just that: open and honest communication where people share their genuine feelings and concerns with each other. Managing conflict is about addressing conflict, and not necessarily about resolving conflict.

Experiencing Conflict in a Hospitable Space

Conflict can be healthy and growth-producing when it is experienced in a hospitable space—a space where there is a commitment to mutual encouragement, creative affirmation of gifts, and love and care for each other as forgiven people in Christ Jesus. Through communicating congruently, claiming your own personal power, listening attentively, and nurturing your own and each other's self-esteem, you can create a hospitable space. If Walt and Laura had continued their conversation and talked with each other in a caring way about what had occurred, they might have been able to create a hospitable space where mutual care, support, and encouragement might have been able to be expressed.

As a church staff, we are called to live as the forgiven community in Christ and create a hospitable space for conflict and growth. If we experience conflict in a hospitable space, we, like Walt and Laura, could improve our relationships with each other and model new ways of relating to the rest of our staff, church, and societal community. As is typical in many staff conflicts, Walt and Laura's conflict arose from a difference in attitudes, expectations, and power or control needs. When (not if) conflicts develop in staff relationships, they may be transformed into creative opportunities for growth by dialoging. If Walt and Laura had begun talking about their feelings concerning what occurred between them, the conflict could have led to their developing a closer, more life-giving relationship.

On a theoretical level, we all know that dialoging about our feelings and expectations in situations of conflict can lead to growth and increased closeness and understanding of each other. Yet on a practical level, the question becomes how can we actually create a hospitable space for conflict, dialog, and growth in our staff relationships.

Four beginning points for creating a hospitable place for conflict are: (1) taking risks; (2) building trust; (3) congruent and honest sharing; and (4) negotiating.

Taking Risks

We are often afraid of being vulnerable or taking risks with each other. Being able to take risks within a staff relationship means being able to directly confront each other with wants, needs, and problems.

Are you able to say directly to other staff what you need or want from them? Are you able to admit that you have made a mistake, that something is wrong, that you have a problem? Do you and the others in your staff pretend everything is fine when inwardly you are hurting?

In order to solve staff problems, we as a staff must be willing to allow each other to state our wants and needs. We must be willing to give up old patterns, ideas, and concepts that are no longer working positively, and be willing to develop new ones and to live as forgiven, faithful, people in Christ Jesus.

Building Trust

What so often precludes us from taking risks is a lack of trust. How do we give ourselves permission to listen and to give up old patterns? It is all a matter of trust, and trust is key to the underlying purpose of covenanting. In covenanting with one another, we need to focus on building trust and on creating a hospitable space in which to communicate congruently and honestly.

Congruent and Honest Sharing

Honest sharing is when we are able to talk openly with each other about both positive and negative feelings which we are experiencing. Such openness enhances the quality of collegial relationships. When we share frustrations and hurts openly with each other, our relationships are strengthened. Direct and honest communication enables painful feelings to be shared rather than bottled up. Open sharing can be done through "I feel" statements rather than "You are" or "You make me feel." For example, Walt would be sharing in a healthy and open manner if he said, "I feel angry when you do Todd and Karee's work before my work," rather than putting Laura on the defensive by saying, "You make me angry when you do their work first," or "You are incompetent." Telling staff members about our problems with them by using "you are" or "you make me" statements results in their defenses being raised. Healthy conversations result when we reveal our own feelings and discuss where we are coming from, rather than placing the blame for our feelings on what we perceive has been done to us.

Congruent communication is vital as we seek to manage conflict in our staff relationships. As discussed in Chapter 10, we all have a tendency toward a particular negative communication style. During times of conflict, we are more likely to "slip" into one of these negative communication styles. Creating a hospitable place for conflict means working hard to avoid:

- placating by giving up our feelings and needs;
- blaming others for the conflict and problem;
- becoming overly reasonable so that we ignore our needs and our co-workers' needs; and
- deciding that the conflict is totally irrelevant to us, our co-workers, and the whole situation.

As we discover which negative communication style fits each of us, we are better able to avoid these unhealthy communication styles and work toward becoming more effective, healthy, and congruent communicators.

In our conversations with our co-workers, we need to clearly articulate our particular needs, interests, ideas, and thoughts. Creating hospitable space also means giving sensitive and careful attention to our co-workers' inner thoughts and feelings, as well as being in tune with our own inner thoughts and feelings. Good eye contact is also vital. Our words need to match our feelings so that our feelings, words, eye contact, gestures, tone of voice, and body language are all congruent with each other.

Negotiating

Negotiating is talking openly and honestly, listening, responding, and compromising when necessary. It is interaction with all participants involved in the conversation. The goal is to reach a decision that is mutually satisfactory and agreeable. When you are negotiating with your staff members, you are not engaged in a win/lose situation but rather in a situation in which all participants are satisfied with the final decision. Negotiating a hospitable space is often described as consensus decision making.

Because of her placating role, her unresolved issues about her own father, and her perception that Todd would not listen but lecture her, Karee rarely tried to negotiate with Todd. In the situation presented at the beginning of Chapter 1, Karee was trying to talk Todd into considering a few changes in the worship service. Neither listened to the other. They fought, and both left angry.

In seeking to negotiate, Karee would have broached the subject to Todd in a different way. She would have said, "I would like to consider having lay people read lessons. What do you think?" Todd, in his new negotiating role, would say, "I'm not crazy about the idea. We've tried it before and it hasn't worked. What do you want to do about this?" Karee would then respond to his questions with her ideas. Todd would listen, and they would come to a decision where both of them could be satisfied with the solution. In this case, perhaps Todd could agree to ask lay people to read lessons on one Sunday of every month. Karee would be satisfied that Todd had listened to her input and Todd would feel his opinions had been respected.

Identifying and Managing Conflict

Utilizing congruent communication skills, the following techniques suggested by Speed Leas are helpful in identifying and managing conflict:[3]

1. Establish boundaries.
2. Structure the process.

3. Search together for common goals.
4. Respond to threats with descriptions and statements of your position.
5. Bring in a third party.

This model for managing conflict can be a way to "work through" conflicts so that when we are engaged in conflict, we feel empowered to choose the outcome of the conflicts together.[4] By means of congruent communication, boundaries, goals, and concerns can be addressed and renegotiated when necessary.

As a member of a church staff, how have you successfully managed conflict in your staff relationships? What are positive aspects of how you have managed conflict? What are the negative things that you have done in situations of staff conflict? What are conflict management skills that you would like to further develop?

As a part of creatively managing conflict, a church staff needs to look at what it means to be members of a faithful, forgiven community that is called to "love one another." To "love one another" in a church staff is to risk being honest with each other about concerns and to work toward trusting one another.

Staff conflicts, like Walt's conflict with Laura, have the potential for motivating problem solving, building up the sense of community among the staff, and reminding each staff member that we are forgiven, faithful people in Christ. As people who seek to love one another in Christ, we are empowered by the Holy Spirit to face conflicts, trust one another, and be honest and vulnerable with each other about who we are.

Thus the question in church staff conflict situations goes beyond "How do we solve this problem?" to the deeper question of "Who are we?" And the answer is clear and succinct: We are faithful people in Christ. Saint Paul states the scriptural basis for church identity: "Abraham *believed*" (Romans 4:3). Faith is the core of our identity as Christians and our identity as church staff members. Who we are is not defined by denomination or title, by name or family. Who we are is not determined by any external boundaries, for any such definition only serves to limit us. Rather who we are as a people and a community is known by our common focus: Jesus Christ. We are a people who share a common belief in the forgiveness which comes through the life, death, and resurrection of Jesus Christ. Our lives are centered on the cross of Christ.

When staff identity is defined in terms of centering rather than binding, a powerful reframing of the concept of forgiveness is also possible. Appearing to the disciples in the closed room, the resurrected Christ breathed on them and said, "Receive the Holy Spirit. If you forgive the sins of any, they are forgiven; if you retain the sins of any, they are retained" (John 20:23). This verse is often isolated from its context and used, in conjunction with Matthew's "office of the keys," as the authorizing of the church with the power to forgive or not forgive sins. A closer look at the context gives a different perspective. Jesus also said, in v. 21, that he sent the disciples out even as the Father had sent him. According to the well-known verses in the third chapter of John, the way of the Father is love ("For God so loved the world . . ."), and the purpose is "not to condemn the world, but that the world might be saved" through the One who is love, the One who embodies forgiveness. A faithful reading, then, lifts up the people called to mission as already forgiven, and sent not to condemn but to bring God's peace to those who believe.

The church staff centered on Christ is a forgiven—already justified and freed in Christ—community. Our empowerment to be a forgiven, faithful staff is not based on our actions, but on the actions of Christ. Through believing and interacting with our staffs as forgiven, faithful people, the role of conflict in our staff communities is set in the positive and life-giving context of commitment and trust.

We, like Walt, need to live out our conflict in the context of faithfulness in Christ. As already forgiven people who center our lives on the death and resurrection of Christ for the forgiveness of our sins, we as staff members need to frame our conflicts in the context of who Christ is for each of us individually and as a staff community. Seeing ourselves as faithful, forgiven staff members, we can then discuss our conflicts with each other honestly, with care and trust.

Forgiving others, and relating with others as forgiven people, is not easy. John Patton, author of *Is Human Forgiveness Possible?*, said forgiveness is sometimes difficult because we mistakenly understand it as something that we may possess. Patton suggested that we need to find ways to understand forgiveness that are less closely related to our defensiveness and sinfulness. We need to begin looking at righteousness in light of the Old Testament image of "right relationship." Being right so as to prove something (often a source of staff conflicts) can serve as a substitute for developing effective relationships. It may also result from our inability to believe that a meaningful relationship with God and each other can really be possible.[5]

Walt and Laura could have gotten lost in a debate about who was right. (Did Walt tell Laura the letters were timely? Did Laura forget about the letters or make the wrong decision about her secretarial priorities?) Yet the question for us as a faithful, forgiven staff is not who is right, but how can we set right our relationship with each other before God.

God's call to us to live in a right relationship with each other is a call to live in a context of forgiveness, the forgiven-ness already mediated by Christ. In our staff relationships, our task is to imitate God's action for us in the way we relate with each other.[6] We imitate God's action for us and we establish a life-giving and hospitable space whereby we all can experience conflict together when we relate with our staff and parish community as people in Christ Jesus who are, as we indeed are, already forgiven people.

Destructive conflict does exist and may often damage and possibly destroy staff relationships. If, however, the staff's identity is centered on the crucified and risen Christ, such conflict can serve to enhance the staff's experience of trust and forgiveness, and may ultimately enhance their staff relationship. If the staff's identity is not focused on the forgiveness of Christ for them, it is more likely that their conflicts will become death-dealing rather than life-giving.

To live as a forgiven person, as a forgiven staff, within the forgiven parish community, means to live and work in an open relationship of commitment to the gospel's imperative of love and respect. Blaming, faultfinding, and labeling have no place in these relationships, as they are symptoms of a deeper problem. They are indications of our inability to accept responsibility for our decisions and manage conflict honestly, and to trust in the forgiveness which is already ours in Christ. To not accept that we are forgiven, healed, and holy people in Christ Jesus is to not accept that Jesus Christ died for us for the forgiveness of our sins. Unless we believe that we are truly forgiven, we are not believing in the new life of the gospel. God calls us to model this personal forgiven-ness in our staff relationships and to celebrate that Jesus truly died and rose for us!

As members of church staffs, we are people who are baptized in Christ Jesus and bound together in faith. We are also people who struggle with our roles, our expectations, and negative communication styles. We are people who strive to strengthen our self-esteem, our sense of personal power, and our skills in communicating congruently.

To believe and know ourselves as the community of forgiven people means to reframe the context for all the struggles and conflicts that we experience in our staff relationships and to see Christ as the center and meaning of all our living. With Christ as the core and "end" of our staff relationships, all the various "means" of conflict management, communication and personal development can enliven and enhance staff relationships. Through relating as a Christ-centered, forgiven staff, God's love can empower us to move beyond our experiences of brokenness and alienation, and transform our conflicts with each other into creative possibilities for healthy and faithful staff relationships.

Rainer Maria Rilke had some sage advice: "Do not now seek the answers which cannot be given you because you would not be able to live them. And the point is, to live everything. Live in the questions now. Perhaps you will gradually, without noticing it, live along some distant day into the answer."[7]

APPENDIX

This book is based on a research study of clergy staffs, focusing on gender, birth order, leadership style, understanding of power, and self-esteem. The sample of 40 members of multiple staffs (10 female/male and 10 male/male teams) was homogeneous in that subjects were Caucasian, American-born, full-time, ordained Lutheran clergy with at least one year of work experience together. Subjects were selected from lists of clergy in team ministries supplied by Lutheran bishops. Data collection consisted of face-to-face, in-depth interviews with each subject. The same focused interview guide and the same questions were used in all the interviews. When a staff member asked what was meant by a certain question or statement, I responded by repeating it in the same way. The interviews were transcribed verbatim and coded utilizing qualitative methods. Themes, concepts, and patterns in their staff relationships, self-esteem, power, sex roles, and families of origin became evident in the analysis of the data. Life course perspective, systems theory, and field theory were utilized. Analyzing the data involved examining the themes and patterns that occurred in the interview as well as establishing coding categories for the analysis of themes, concepts, typologies, and interpretations.

The data revealed five primary findings. First, open communication, complementary skills and respect were found to be key components of a "good" team relationship. Second, staff members with high self-esteem had "good" team relationships and staff members with low self-esteem had "poor" relationships. Third, staff members with high self-esteem shared power and had "good" relationships, while teammates with low self-esteem did not share power equally and had "poor" relationships. Fourth, staff members preferred female/male teams because a more complete picture of the people of God was presented, and women offered different skills and personality traits. Women in ministry viewed power as an enabling tool whereas the majority of men in ministry viewed power as a tool of influence and persuasion. Also, women felt that their teammates related with them as daughters or as "surrogate spouses" wherein they experienced pressure to take on the role of emotional supporter in the relationship. Fifth, staff members tended to re-create their families of origin in terms of birth order role, level of closeness, and conflict style. Staff members of different birth orders had better quality relationships than teammates of the same birth order. A relationship between two-, single-, and substitute-parent families and the quality of the staff relationships was found in that staffs which ranked as "poor" had one member who grew up in a single- or substitute-parent family. Ethnicity influenced the majority of staff members in terms of their own expression of feelings and affections, piety, self-worth, and stability.

If you are interested in reading further about the research objectives, design, methodology, analysis of data, findings, and conclusions, my dissertation, *Multiple Staff Clergy Relationships* (copyright © 1987), is available through the library at Texas Women's Unversity in Denton, Texas, and the library at Wartburg Theological Seminary in Dubuque, Iowa.

NOTES

Chapter 2: Relating as a Faithful and Forgiven Staff

1. Delbert R. Hillers, *Covenant: The History of a Biblical Idea* (Baltimore: The Johns Hopkins University Press, 1969), p. 168.

2. Letty Russell, *The Future of Partnership* (Philadelphia: Westminster Press, 1979), p. 176.

3. Presentation by Dr. Paul Bauermeister, Christ Seminary-Seminex Professor at Lutheran School of Theology in Chicago.

4. Norman E. Wegmeyer, *Strengthening the Multiple Staff* (Minneapolis: Augsburg, 1982), pp. 12-13.

Chapter 3: Identifying Role and Staff Expectations

1. Anne Wilson Schaef, *Women's Reality: An Emerging Female System in the White Male Society* (Minneapolis: Winston Press, 1981), pp. 104-5.

2. Ibid., pp. 120-22.

Chapter 4: Discovering Family and Staff Similarities

1. Irene Goldenberg and Harold Goldenberg, *Family Therapy: An Overview* (Monterey, Calif.: Brooks/Cole Publishing Co., 1980), p. 3.

2. Ibid., pp. 29-31.

Chapter 5: Determining Your Family and Staff Roles

1. Goldenberg and Goldenberg, *Family Therapy*, p. 20.

2. Walter Toman, *Family Constellation* (New York: Springer Publishing Co., 1976).

3. Lyle E. Schaller, *The Multiple Staff and the Local Church* (Nashville: Abingdon Press, 1980), p. 102.

4. Ibid., p. 101.

5. Toman, pp. 9-11.

6. Ibid., p. 179.
7. Ibid., p. 167.

Chapter 6: Understanding Your Personality

1. Isabel Briggs Myers, *Gifts Differing* (Palo Alto, Calif.: Consulting Psychologists Press, Inc., 1980), p. 54.
2. Ibid., pp. 5-6, 31-48, 57-63.
3. Ibid., pp. 3-4.
4. David Keirsey and Marilyn Bates, *Please Understand Me* (Del Mar, Calif.: Promethean Books, Inc., 1978), pp. 25-26.
5. Gary Harbaugh, *God's Gifted People* (Minneapolis: Augsburg, 1988).

Chapter 7: Strengthening Your Self-Esteem

1. J. Battle, *The Culture-Free Self-Esteem Inventories for Children and Adults* (Seattle: Special Child Publishing, 1981).
2. D. S. Ryan, "Self-Esteem: An Operational Definition and Ethical Analysis," in *Journal of Psychology and Theology* 11(1983): 295-302.
3. Pete Bradford, *The Management of Self-Esteem* (Englewood Cliffs, N.J.: Prentice-Hall, 1981), p. 6.

Chapter 8: Recognizing Your Power

1. Russell, The *Future of Partnership*, p. 137.
2. Schaef, *Women's Reality*, p. 125.

Chapter 10: Discovering Your Negative Communication Styles

1. Virginia Satir, *Peoplemaking* (Palo Alto, Calif.: Science and Behavior Books, 1972), p. 59.
2. Ibid.

Chapter 11: Becoming a Congruent Communicator

1. Satir, *Peoplemaking*, p. 59.

Chapter 12: Managing Conflict in a Forgiving Community

1. Jean Baker Miller, *Toward a New Psychology of Women* (Boston: Beacon Press, 1976), p. 125.
2. C. Douglass Lewis, *Resolving Church Conflicts: A Case Study Approach for Local Congregations* (New York: Harper & Row, 1981), p. 15.
3. Speed Leas, *Leadership and Conflict* (Creative Leadership Series) (Nashville: Abingdon Press, 1982), p. 101.

4. Ibid., p. 114.

5. John Patton, *Is Human Forgiveness Possible? A Pastoral Care Perspective* (Nashville: Abingdon Press, 1985), pp. 90, 114.

6. Ibid., p. 153.

7. Rainer Maria Rilke, *Letters to a Young Poet*, quoted in Russell, *The Future of Partnership*, p. 156.

FOR FURTHER READING_____

Block, Peter. *The Empowered Manager.* San Francisco: Jossey-Bass, Inc., Publishers, 1987.

Bloomfield, Harold H. *Making Peace with Your Parents.* New York: Random House, 1983.

Bromson, Robert M. *Coping with Difficult People.* New York: Ballantine Books, 1981.

Friedman, Edwin H. *Generation to Generation.* New York: The Guilford Press, 1985.

Goldenberg, Irene, and Harold Goldenberg. *Family Therapy.* Monterey, Calif.: Brooks/Cole Publishing Co., 1980.

Gutek, Barbara A. *Sex and the Workplace.* San Francisco: Jossey-Bass Publishers, 1985.

Harbaugh, Gary L. *The Faith-Hardy Christian.* Minneapolis: Augsburg, 1986.

_____. *God's Gifted People.* Minneapolis: Augsburg, 1988.

_____. *Pastor as Person.* Minneapolis: Augsburg, 1984.

Hillers, Delbert R. *Covenant: The History of a Biblical Idea.* Baltimore: The Johns Hopkins Press, 1969.

Hulme, William F. *Pastors in Ministry.* Minneapolis: Augsburg, 1985.

Jung, C. G. *Psychological Types.* Princeton, N.J.: Princeton University Press, 1971.

Leas, Speed. *Leadership and Conflict.* Creative Leadership Series. Nashville: Abingdon Press, 1982.

Lerner, Harriet Goldhor. *Dance of Anger.* New York: Harper & Row, 1985.

Lewis, C. Douglass. *Resolving Church Conflicts: A Case Study Approach for Local Congregations.* New York: Harper & Row, 1981.

McGoldrick, Monica. *Genograms in Family Assessment.* New York: W. W. Norton & Co., 1985.

Miller, Jean Baker. *Toward a New Psychology of* Women. Boston: Beacon Press, 1976.

Myers, Isabel Briggs. *Gifts Differing.* Palo Alto, Calif.: Consulting Psychologists Press, Inc., 1980.

Osborne, Cecil G. *Self-Esteem: Overcoming Inferiority Feelings.* Nashville: Abingdon Press, 1986.

Patton, John. *Is Human Forgiveness Possible? A Pastoral Care Perspective.* Nashville: Abingdon Press, 1985.

Sanford, Linda Tshirhart and Mary Ellen Donovan. *Women and Self-Esteem.* Baltimore: Penquin Books, 1984.

Satir, Virginia. *Peoplemaking.* Palo Alto, Calif.: Science and Behavior Books, 1972.

Schaef, Anne Wilson. *Co-Dependence.* New York: Harper & Row, 1986.

_____. *Women's Reality: An Emerging Female System in the White Male Society.* Minneapolis: Winston Press, Inc., 1981.

Toman, Walter. *Family Constellation.* 3rd ed. New York: Springer Pub. Co., 1976.

Tournier, Paul. *The Whole Person in a Broken World.* New York: Harper & Row, 1964.

Voydanoff, Patricia. *Work and Family: Changing Roles of Men and Women.* Palo Alto, Calif.: Mayfield Pub. Co., 1984.

Watzlawick, Paul, Janet Beavin Bavelas, and Dan D. Jackson. *Pragmatics of Human Communication.* New York: W. W. Norton & Co., 1967.

Young-Eisendrath, Polly. *Female Authority.* New York: The Guilford Press, 1987.